Hope you enjoy
the Book
Tay Feejr

# AN
# *Oasis*
## IN THE WILDERNESS

TONY FERRIGNO

Copyright © 2018 Tony Ferrigno.

All rights reserved. No part of this book may be used or reproduced by any means, graphic, electronic, or mechanical, including photocopying, recording, taping or by any information storage retrieval system without the written permission of the author except in the case of brief quotations embodied in critical articles and reviews.

LifeRich Publishing is a registered trademark of The Reader's Digest Association, Inc.

LifeRich Publishing books may be ordered through booksellers or by contacting:

LifeRich Publishing
1663 Liberty Drive
Bloomington, IN 47403
www.liferichpublishing.com
1 (888) 238-8637

Because of the dynamic nature of the Internet, any web addresses or links contained in this book may have changed since publication and may no longer be valid. The views expressed in this work are solely those of the author and do not necessarily reflect the views of the publisher, and the publisher hereby disclaims any responsibility for them.

Any people depicted in stock imagery provided by Getty Images are models, and such images are being used for illustrative purposes only. Certain stock imagery © Getty Images.

ISBN: 978-1-4897-1653-8 (sc)
ISBN: 978-1-4897-1652-1 (hc)
ISBN: 978-1-4897-1651-4 (e)

Library of Congress Control Number: 2018939268

Print information available on the last page.

LifeRich Publishing rev. date: 08/13/2018

This book is dedicated to my daughter Kathleen, whom I love very dearly and for whom I will always have a very special place in my heart.

## ACKNOWLEDGEMENT:

I'd like to thank my good friend and editor, Holly Weiss, for all her help in putting this book together with me. Without her assistance, I may have still been writing and scratching my head.

# CONTENTS

Foreword: Recovery International at 80: The
          Effectiveness of a Little-Known Program
          (by: Marilyn Schmitt, PhD) ............................................... xv
Prologue: How the Recovery Inc. Self-Help Model
          Brought Me Peace (An Oasis in the Wilderness)
          (by: Tony Ferrigno) .......................................................... xvii

## PART 1
### MY STORY: BEFORE, DURING AND TWILIGHT YEARS OF RECOVERY

Chapter 1:  Dealing With Stress on the Job ........................................ 1
Chapter 2:  Dealing with Family Stress ............................................. 13
Chapter 3:  Discovering Recovery and Hawaii Vacation ................. 21
Chapter 4:  History of the Origin of Recovery .................................. 28
Chapter 5:  Taking on Local Recovery Responsibilities and
               the Chicago Tour ............................................................ 39
Chapter 6:  Taking on More Responsibilities From Recovery
               International .................................................................... 42
Chapter 7:  Strategic Planning (Getting Recovery Back on
               its Feet Again) ................................................................. 50
Chapter 8:  Controversies, Stones and Setback ................................ 56
Chapter 9:  The Twilight Years and the Sadness ............................. 65
Chapter 10: The Three, Me and Recovery ......................................... 78
Chapter 11: The Misconceptions of Mental Illness and the
               Stigma That Follows (Educating the Patient as
               Well as Society) .............................................................. 92

# PART 2

Chapter 12: What is The Recovery Method and What is Cognitive Behavioral Therapy?..................97
Chapter 13: Comparison of Cognitive Behavioral Therapy (CBT) and The Recovery Method (RM)..................110
Chapter 14: Who Thought of CBT and How Did it Originate?....118
Chapter 15: Discussions on Mental Health Topics From the CBT Networking For Professional Therapists Website..................128
- Exceptionality
- How do you help patients accept uncertainty?
- Right or Wrong
- Making ourselves RIGHT and others WRONG seems to be one of the principal ego-mind patterns. Any suggestion on how one can consciously change this pattern for a more fulfilling life?
- Anxiety
- "Physical illness and mental illness. Why is there a separation? Or, is there a separation?"
- Not able to focus, gets into thoughts in a conversation and feels bad about himself, does it seem to be ADD? Suggestions appreciated.
- I have a young man with PTSD, severe explosive tendencies and agoraphobia, social anxiety.
- Temper
- Thoughts: Racing thoughts in bipolar disorders
- OCD patients and good exercises for intrusive thoughts (a lot of "should've" feelings)
- Where do our "thoughts" come from?
- Anxiety: A therapist asked if we can come up with some strategies that can be used for those dealing with anxiety and if we can recommend resources

- Stigma: This is about a client thinking about whether it's ridiculous to tell her boyfriend that she's dealing with bipolar disorder.
- When fear presents itself as a "sick feeling" in the stomach

Chapter 16: Recovery Method Mental Health Tools to Live By....156
- Nervous symptoms and self-diagnosing
- Temper
- Temperamental (extreme) language
- Learning what we can or cannot control
- Muscle control
- Inner and outer environment
- Inner and outer approval
- Exceptionality
- Having the courage to make mistakes
- Partial and total viewpoints
- Attacking the weakest link
- Observing and interpreting
- There are no rights or wrongs
- Self-spotting and foreign spotting

"Now let me tell you that I speak to you as your doctor. I speak to you as one who trains you back from sickness to health. '**Mine is a voice crying in the wilderness, except in Recovery. And it's unfortunate that it is so, because outside in the wilderness of cities and towns, I call this** *an oasis,* **and the other** *a wilderness.*' In this wilderness of modern life, they try to teach you that everything is fate, not will. They try to teach you that once you have been frustrated in your childhood, you are doomed, unless some expert steps in and treats you for three or four or five years at a certain fee, which is, of course, considerably extended likewise. Why people should constantly be dragging their youth behind them, I have not been able to realize after I drifted away from this modern teaching."

*Abraham Low, "Manage Your Fears, Manage Your Anger," Lecture 3: Will Versus Fate, pp. 15-16.*

"Recovery stands for simplicity. Its system of instruction and training are meant to enable the plain, humble and untutored patient to practice self-help. An objective of this kind cannot be achieved by means of involved explanations and complex techniques. Self-help in psychiatric after-care calls for simple methods of interpreting and manipulating systems. It is for this reason that Recovery offers to its members plain common sense instead of intricate philosophies and artless techniques of training in place of elaborate procedures."

*A. Low, "Mental Health Through Will-Training," Part 3, Chapter 10, Sabotage Method No. 9: Failure to Practice Muscle Control, p. 262.*

"Understanding alone will not help and has not helped any patient that has developed a long term nervous problem. The only thing that will help the patient is training, persistent training. And how this training is done, I am not going to tell you, but that's what this organization has been built for. And if you want to know how this training is done, my advice is to come and undergo the training, not to get it explained. But once you undergo the training keep in mind a day's training or a week's training is insufficient. And if you only want to spend a limited time on this training program, you better stay out of it."

> *A. Low, "Manage Your Fears, Manage Your Anger,"*
> *Lecture 2: The Passion for Self-Distrust, pp. 9-10.*

"And if a person reaches the stage where he only develops symptoms occasionally, where he develops physical discomfort occasionally, and mental discomfort occasionally, then he is practically well. He has become an average nervous person."

> *A. Low, "Manage Your Fears, Manage Your Anger," Lecture 8: Nervous Patient Versus Nervous Person, p. 44.*

"And don't listen to anybody who will tell you once you have had a severe nervous or mental condition that you will never come back. That's of course arrant nonsense, and don't listen to such prophets of doom."

> *A. Low, "Manage Your Fears, Manage Your Anger," Lecture 12: Intellectual Validity and Romantic Vitality, p.69.*

FOREWORD

# RECOVERY INTERNATIONAL AT 80: THE EFFECTIVENESS OF A LITTLE-KNOWN PROGRAM

*Marilyn Schmitt, PhD*

In 1937 a movement began to be shaped that would improve the lives of many thousands of people suffering from mental and nervous disorders. The movement became a group-based training protocol developed by a Chicago neuropsychiatrist, Abraham Low, MD. In the heyday of Freudian psychoanalysis, Low saw his patients in the University of Illinois Psychiatric Research Hospital discharged and returning in a revolving door of relapse. He began to experiment with tools that would train them to manage their symptoms and develop resistance to the illness. And he founded an "association of patients," choosing the word "Recovery" as its name. Today its name is Recovery International.

Fifteen years after that beginning, in 1952, the program was complete: a group-based, peer-led cognitive behavioral training program that has enabled tens of thousands of sufferers from mental and nervous disorders to achieve peaceful, productive, and normal lives. Today, with hundreds of weekly group meetings across North America and abroad, led without required fee by trained volunteer former sufferers, Recovery International is the "best kept secret in the psychotherapeutic world."

The Recovery International System uses highly structured meetings in which participants describe a disturbing everyday event, their reaction to it, and their coping strategy, ending with acknowledgement of their improvement compared to the past. The group then comments on the story using the principles, concepts, and language established by Abraham Low. This deceptively simple format continually restructures the thinking and behavior of each individual at whatever pace that person can achieve. Readings and other resources reinforce this "getting well" process. Between-meeting practice of the principles is constantly stressed.

The Department of Psychiatry of the University of Illinois-Chicago has just concluded a study of 126 participants, most with a long-standing serious disorder, attending Recovery International meetings. The study concludes that after one year of attendance, most subjects experienced significant reduction of depressive and anxiety symptoms as well as decreased domination by symptoms. They were using fewer mental health and social services and displayed increased coping skills, self-esteem, and feelings of hope. The more meetings they attended, the more benefit they experienced. (See the Report at www.recoveryinternational.org.)

In a 1973 issue of *Psychiatric News,* Karl Menninger publicly expressed regret that he had not paid attention to Recovery International. He spoke of "legions of people whose lives were saved or fulfilled by" this self-help organization. How many more legions have been saved since then, and yet the Low System remains a secret to the vast majority of mental health professionals and the public.

As Recovery International celebrated its 80th anniversary in 2017, it is time for that disregard to come to an end, for consumers and professionals alike. The Low System, as delivered in Recovery International meetings, offers a time tested, broad-based, low - cost and now verified benefit to those suffering from mental and nervous disorders. Learn more about Recovery International and other Low System-based programs at www.recoveryinternational.org

PROLOGUE

# HOW THE RECOVERY INC. SELF-HELP MODEL BROUGHT ME PEACE (AN OASIS IN THE WILDERNESS)

*Tony Ferrigno*

It was during the late 1980s, having been employed as an ironworker for 25 years, that I began to develop both physical and mental stress. My parents' health declined and eventually they died. Enormous stress forced me to retire on disability. I started experiencing intense and debilitating physical symptoms. I didn't know why, but I was more nervous than ever. This nervousness brought on difficulty breathing, stomach upset and a lot of pain on my side. The thought of meeting people who might notice my condition only increased my symptoms. Eventually I avoided leaving the house

My life was changing rapidly. Going to church was an ordeal and traveling on buses, trains and planes far away from home was out of the question.

I began thinking if this is the way I had to live, maybe life wasn't worth living. These thoughts terrified me no end. How could I end my life when I had a family, a wife and kids? What about them? I felt there was no way out. How would I survive?

Desperate for relief, but undecided about whether to consult a medical doctor or therapist, I scheduled an appointment with both. My family doctor couldn't find anything wrong physically and advised that it was probably my nerves that were causing my symptoms. The psychotherapist confirmed the same, recommending therapy sessions and a referral to a psychiatrist so that medication could be prescribed.

Eventually, I began to feel some relief. Then one day a cousin told me about a self-help organization that she had consulted several years before when she had started to undergo panic attacks. She asserted, "Of all the doctors I went to and all the medication I took, the one thing that helped me the most was Recovery Inc."

I decided to try it. I attended several meetings in my neighborhood and heard people describe similar experiences with nervous symptoms. It was incredible to hear how life had changed so dramatically for them once they found Recovery Inc. They had gotten well even though initially they could not leave their homes, had stayed in bed most of the time, had been hospitalized often, and had even attempted suicide. I thought if they could do it, so could I.

Determined that this was the program for me, I continued to attend meetings regularly, studying and learning what was known as the Recovery "Method." More important than just knowing the Method was to practice it. Of course, when one attempts to do something that he fears and hates to do, he most certainly will be uncomfortable. But the Recovery Method taught us that our health improved by the amount of discomfort we were willing to bear. We understood that our symptoms were distressing but not dangerous. The things we feared and hated to do were the everyday things the average person does. Thus many of us turned what was once a vicious cycle of helplessness into a vitalizing cycle of self-confidence.

Since, like me, so many individuals first learn about Recovery Inc. through word of mouth, it is surprising to discover that this self-help organization based in Chicago, Illinois has existed since 1937. Approximately 700 free, weekly, community-based group fellowship meetings are run throughout the United States and abroad, including 30 groups right here in New York City.

The founder of Recovery Inc. and its unique results-oriented Method was the late Dr. Abraham A. Low, an accomplished and successful neuropsychiatrist. Dr. Low carefully formulated the simple Recovery Method of will training (which employed what was later identified as a cognitive behavioral approach) to achieve emotional and mental health.

Realizing that most of the patients routinely suffered distressing symptoms, he taught that they could, in fact, continue to function by accepting their symptoms as merely distressing but not dangerous. The language and behavior of the patients changed as they learned to practice disciplined control of their defeatist thinking and undesirable impulses.

Soon after discovering Recovery Inc. in 1990, I began to feel better. I undertook leadership training, volunteering my time to do whatever I could to help those out there suffering needlessly and quietly as I had been. I have since opened three Recovery groups in Brooklyn and continue to work tirelessly to identify prospective leaders within our groups to open more groups.

As of January 2002, I became the Area Leader for New York City. My goal is to open as many doors as I can to reach out to both consumers and the professional community, along with other volunteers and non-profit mental health organizations.

# PART 1

*My Story: Before, During and Twilight Years of Recovery*

# CHAPTER 1

# DEALING WITH STRESS ON THE JOB

An unusual turn of events in my life occurred was when I left the employ of the New York City Transit Authority (TA) and began working for the New York City Department of Transportation (DOT) as an ironworker. The actual title was Bridgeman and Riveter, later changed to Bridge Repairer and Riveter. I had thought that I would retire from the TA; but as things happen in life, there are times when the unexpected occurs. There were applications from the DOT seeking to hire ironworkers for the Bridge Department. I had occasionally heard talk about this popular job, which paid prevailing wages, what union ironworkers received on the outside construction jobs. These wages were one and a half times more than what I was making in the TA. At that time (1973-1974), I had a wife and three young kids and was having a hard time making ends meet. I had been thinking of working a second job for awhile when unexpectedly the DOT job became available.

I filed an application, took the test and passed it. The next thing I knew, I was hired. As much as I wanted to make this extra money, I felt I really didn't want to leave the job I had at the TA. It meant leaving all the friends I had and got along with very well. I was content there and was also on a list to become a foreman. I knew the people I would be working with in the DOT would mostly be outside union ironworkers. How would I get along with them? I never worked on outside construction jobs, let alone on city bridges. Would they be tough working with, or was I making more out of it than I should? I wished some of my friends with whom I worked had taken the test, passed, and maybe could have joined me on my new venture. Unfortunately, none of them applied and at times I would be wondering why. It's crazy sometimes how you think. Here I felt I was the kind of guy who would be most apprehensive about this new job and working with men about whom I wasn't so sure. What about them? Could they have felt as apprehensive as I did? Could be, who knew? In any case, I took the job and just hoped it would turn out to be okay.

We worked in five locations throughout the city. I was assigned to the Brooklyn Bridge shop located under the Manhattan Bridge, which we also serviced. The foreman there was a drinker who appeared to be a pretty nice guy. In the beginning I got along with him fairly well, but after several months I saw his true colors. One of the fellows I came to like a lot was Joe, the kind of guy I wish everyone could be like. As time passed, unfortunately he was the only person with whom I felt comfortable. The others never seemed to be down-to-earth. They weren't necessarily bad guys, but there was a certain pretense about them that bothered me. I always felt I had to be careful about what I would say, since I was the only one there who didn't do ironwork on outside construction. I would hear them talk about some of their previous jobs and there was quite a bit of bolstering and laughter. The laughter most of the time, never seemed sincere; it seemed more designed to fit in with the pack. I was not used to that, so I basically remained silent and just listened occasionally, laughing a bit.

One day the foreman came upstairs into our locker room. He had been drinking and thought he would have a little fun teasing Joe, who he did not like because Joe's brother-in-law was the foreman at the Brooklyn Williamsburg Bridge shop, and he didn't like him either.

## AN OASIS IN THE WILDERNESS

The foreman would threaten Joe in different ways that could have possibly gotten Joe fired. Joe was really a very nice person but seemed to have a lot of bad luck, not only in his personal life but on the job as well. I remember one of the men saying, "If Joe didn't have all this bad luck, he wouldn't have any luck at all." This day the boss saw I was sitting next to Joe and said, "You're always with him." I said, "So, we work together and you assign us the jobs, so why wouldn't I be with Joe often?" He didn't like that and now I felt I was on his crap list. When I entered the locker room the following morning, Joe and some of the others were talking about the prior day's incident. Some were trying to calm him down because he was so angry about the boss. He felt he had had enough of the foreman and wanted to tell the supervising engineer that he was being threatened by him.

At this point, I approached Joe and tried to tell him I didn't think it was such a good idea either and that it might come back to haunt him in the future. He said he didn't care and nothing was going to stop him. With that I said, "In that case, I want to go along with you to verify what you're saying." I continued, "As a matter of fact, he threatened me also and maybe it's best we say something now rather than wait until it may be too late." Joe didn't argue with me. When we spoke to the super-engineer, both of us discussed only the one incident, the foreman threatening us. We could have spoken about a lot more that we knew could have brought him a whole lot of trouble, but we didn't. We knew if anything more were to come of this situation we would have to wait for it to occur and, if necessary, we could always bring it up then. As it turned out, nothing formally happened, and the situation was just left in our heads to ponder from time to time.

Some of the jobs we did were somewhat nerve-racking and scary. One incident also became a bit interesting and humorous. We had to walk up the main cables on the Brooklyn Bridge and repair some cable wires that had broken. Wearing our safety belts, we made it to the top of the Brooklyn tower and completed the job. When we began to walk back down the cables, we noticed there was no traffic at all in either the Brooklyn or Manhattan lanes. Then we saw a reporter's car from one of the TV networks with a light flashing on top, looking for a story. Once we got down onto the walkway, we were informed that a bystander had called in to report that someone was on the cable and might be seeking to commit suicide. Needless to say, it was a false alarm. We knew the Brooklyn Bridge was historical and the bridge of choice for most of those wanting to commit suicide. What I thought was somewhat funny was, didn't the person who called it in see that we were wearing safety belts, and if someone did want to commit suicide, why would he feel the need for a safety belt? Chalk it up to another "only in New York City" story.

In the early to mid-1970s, the City of New York was experiencing fiscal problems and layoff slips were issued to many City employees. I received one but since I already had over ten years of seniority with the TA, it allowed me to continue working. Some of our men were laid off and because the Williamsburg Bridge shop lost more than most, another fellow worker and I were transferred there. I had mixed feelings. (Years later, I would learn that in Recovery lingo, this was referred to as, "We fear change and hate routine.") I now had to travel a little further to work and get accustomed to a new foreman and coworkers. It wasn't that different, although I did miss having Joe around. But things like that happen and I realized I had better get used to it.

The foreman there was Joe's brother-in-law, the one mentioned earlier. He was a bit on the stuck-up side. He had me work in the shop a lot and when he wasn't around and the phone would ring I had to answer it. I would say "hello" and then wait for the person to speak, taking whatever message was given to me and the person calling. However, on a few occasions I'd forget to get the person's name. When asked by the boss to whom I had spoken, I didn't always remember. This would irritate him and he would lecture me quite a bit. He would insist, "Tony, you have to get the person's name, you have to ask and get the person's name." When he would leave I would think to myself, "I know it's a little frustrating, however, he should understand that I'm not exactly his secretary either. I'm concentrating

## AN OASIS IN THE WILDERNESS

on my work, the phone rings and I run to get it before the person hangs up. So occasionally I don't get the name, so what, what's the big deal?"

One time, a shoefly came around to spy on us, trying to catch us doing something wrong. I happened to be working with a couple of guys in the back of the electricians' shop and took the truck to go a few blocks away to pick up coffee for the guys. It was just about what anyone would do in the early morning. When I returned to our yard the shoefly was there and I knew it wasn't going to look good when I recognized who he was. Sure enough, he approached me and asked where I had just come from. I knew he could see the bag with the coffee and such, so what could I say? "I went to pick up coffee for the guys," I told him. He said, "You used a city truck to get coffee?" "Yes," I said, "it's faster." While he was talking to me one of our guys saw the exchange and thought he'd come over and give him a piece of his mind, so he came out with a couple of wisecracks. I thought, "Oh no, now we're really going to be in trouble." The shoefly took our names down and I found out later that our other men who were going out on the bridge to do a job had stopped off someplace to have their coffee and had also been caught by the same guy. We were all told to report to our head office on Worth St. in the afternoon. My boss came in late that morning and when we told him what had happened, he was fit to be tied. "What did he say to you?" "He asked me where I had just come from." I continued, "I just came back from picking up coffee." Well, that's all my boss needed to hear. He turned to me and said in an angry tone, "You went to pick up coffee, you told him that, why did you say that?" "Well, I knew he could see the bag with the coffee." The boss reiterated, "You don't tell him that. I can't believe you said that to him." Later on in the afternoon everyone including the boss (with the exception of me, because he sent me to pick up the weekly paychecks) had gone to our main office on Worth St. When everyone returned, I asked one of the guys what had happened. "He was angry with all of us, especially when he felt everyone was lying to him and making excuses, except for one person (he meant you). He said that you were the only guy who was honest and told the truth." I laughed and said, "Oh my God, I wish I was there to see the boss's face," and then laughed some more.

As the years were passing I found I still wasn't happy with this job. I wasn't content and wished I had stayed at my former job. When I would think about the time when the layoff slips were sent out maybe I would have been better off had I gotten one rather than the City doing me a favor by keeping me on because of my seniority. It would have given me the opportunity to return to my former job without the embarrassment of going back on my own. I felt going back on my own would have bothered me no end. I would have thought of myself as being somewhat of a coward. I wondered what the guys with whom I was friends would possibly be thinking of me. They most likely would have been happy to see me back; but would they then think of me as less of a person who was fragile and sensitive and not man enough to handle the new job? Even if I did return what about the money?

I would be earning less again and back to the thought of getting a second job. And what about retiring? I might have had the twenty-five years in, but I didn't have the age requirement which would have taken at least nine more years. To me, nine years was forever. It seemed there was no way out. I just had to stick it out and hope for the best.

Another incident occurred that caused some of the foremen to be shifted around. This time we got someone with whom I was happy (well, at least content). He was the kind of guy I wished all the foremen would emulate. He was down-to-earth, respectful and looked out for others. I was invigorated with a new sense of belonging. No sooner did I start to develop a better attitude toward this job when things took another turn for the worse. The same shoefly returned to the shop office to speak with my boss. I could hear a little quarreling but didn't know what it was about. When he left, I asked my boss what had happened. "Ah," he said. "He was being tough with me and telling me how I should be running the job." When I asked, "What did you tell him?" he replied, "I told him to go f_ _k himself." "Wow, you told him that?," I asked, with a bit of a chuckle and smile on my face. He said, "Yeh, he deserves it." He then dropped a bomb on me when he mentioned he was going to be transferred to the 59th St. Bridge shop. "But that's where you had been for years and liked it there." He said, "Yeh, I know, but he doesn't know that." We then laughed and I remarked, "How do you like that, you tell him to go f_ _k himself and he punishes you by sending you back to where you wanted to go all along. Unbelievable!" We laughed again. Well, I was happy for my boss but now felt all the old lousy nerves resurfacing.

Well, well, wouldn't you know it: the foreman who took over our shop was none other than the one I had first begun with, "The Drinker" or, as we used to call him, "Suds." We were back together again. Surprisingly, he brought his sidekick along with him, who fit in quite nicely, as his disciple. He followed in his footsteps with all the conniving and nefarious ways one can think of. We all managed to get along with each other for awhile, since Suds had been planning to retire very soon and, at that point, his sidekick would take over as provisional foreman.

When that day came, the acting foreman took me under his wing somewhat and, as time went on, I thought increasingly of getting away from him. He got into things he shouldn't have been doing. My problem was he was getting me involved in some of them.

One afternoon, he told me that he was going to Manhattan to meet someone and said, "If my wife calls, tell her that I'm working overtime tonight." With that he took off with the pick-up truck. His wife did call and asked to speak with him. I told her, "He's out on a job right now, and he told me to tell you that he would be working overtime tonight." She said, "Okay, thank you," and hung up the phone. I felt terrible lying to her. It was something I had never done before. Shortly after that I received another call, this time from my boss. "Tony, do me a favor. Take my car and drive it to where I'm at." He gave me the name of the bar and location. I did as he said, and when I arrived I entered the bar and saw him sitting and talking with a lady. He asked me to have a seat and ordered a beer for me and introduced me to the lady. We chatted for a few minutes, exchanged car keys, said goodbye and I drove the truck back to the shop. It was an odd experience for me and it made me very uncomfortable and

I kept thinking of what, if anything, I should do about this. Should I just let it go and forget it, or should I say something to him? I just wasn't sure. The next day feeling a little nervous, I went into the office and said to him, "Don't ever ask me to do that again." He looked at me slightly and then nodded his head as if to say "Okay."

When the foreman wasn't around or took the day off I was left in charge. I didn't really care for this, but at least the boss wasn't there. One day while in charge, two of the men left the job site and drove back to the shop. They came into the office and one was coughing and spitting up a lot of blood. I told the other guy to take him immediately to Beekman Downtown Hospital in Manhattan. If I remember correctly, the doctors had a difficult time containing the bleeding but they finally managed to do so. We later heard that he was diagnosed as having cancer. We visited him at Memorial Sloan Kettering Hospital where he was receiving chemotherapy. He had a long struggle battling the disease and at times it appeared that he was losing the battle. He used all of his sick time and was now receiving partial pay. There had been some hope for awhile that he would pull through but that was short lived. It now seemed we were going to get the news soon that he passed away.

This thing with my boss was really annoying me terribly, causing me to request that I be sent out on jobs with the rest of the gang. He granted this, and I felt a little sense of relief. I would not enjoy working with most of the gang due to their own foibles; however, I felt I needed to distance myself from the boss as much as possible. I needed a little fresh air.

The majority of our work focused on repairs to the Williamsburg Bridge, and we also repaired highways and overpasses. Part of our job was also hanging wooden scaffolding under the roadways which enabled us to get to the iron structure that needed repairing. One day we were working on one of these scaffolds beneath the roadway of the Williamsburg Bridge. I was working with a burning torch, another guy was welding and while we were doing our job, there were also bridge painters painting off of the same scaffolding we were on. It was a bit ridiculous for us all to be situated within such close proximity of each other. It was not too unusual working under these conditions as there were many other jobs that we did that didn't make much sense at the time. It was par for the course. While using the burning torch, some sparks flew into the five gallon paint can. When I looked over and to my surprise, there was a flame coming out of the bucket, I shut off the torch and went over to the burning bucket. I thought, "Okay, how should I put this fire out? I could maybe smother it, I guess." Then it struck me: "Why not just kick it off the scaffold? Simple, that's the East River below with all that water." It made sense to me so I did just that. I kicked it off the side and down it went, hitting the water and creating a big splash, disappearing below the surface. As I looked I saw there was no longer a flame. "Great," I thought, "that takes care of that." A moment later while still looking down below, I couldn't believe what I was seeing. It was a flame floating on the water. As I watched in disbelief, it was floating in a northerly direction and toward the Domino Sugar facility.

I also saw a large cargo tanker docked at the pier. Now my heart was racing and my imagination was literally on fire. Would it hit the ship and, if anything like grease, oil or gasoline were possibly on the ship's surface, would it explode? If I tried going up on the roadway jump in the truck and raced over there, it would be too late. My racing thoughts were, "Oh my God, this could be a catastrophe." I could see it all over the evening news with me trying to explain what happened. Would anybody be killed or injured? I just kept having those awful thoughts. As things turned out, one of our guys who was up on the roadway did jump into a truck and drove down to the sugar plant and spoke with some guys there who saw the flames floating toward the area. "The flames died out by the time it hit anything," they said. Thank God, no one got hurt or lost their lives. Then a funny thought came to mind: "Oh well, so much for being on the Six o'clock News."

It was beginning to be a struggle getting up in the morning and reporting to work, but I just kept on pushing myself and hoping for the better up until the day I reported for work and was standing in the office. And then it happened. Here entered the guy who we all figured would die before ever returning back to work. To me it felt like the Twilight Zone. "Are you kidding me?" I said to myself. "Here I am hoping and praying I can get out of here and who, of all people, comes walking in? None other than the guy we figured was on his death bed and who we probably would never see again." Here he was, someone who couldn't wait to get back to work again. I thought, "He has all the best of reasons for not being here and yet, here he is." This was a situation when one wanted to welcome a person back to work, which we did, but in my mind I thought, "What is he thinking? And how am I going to make it through the day, let alone tomorrow and after that?"

Considering all the stress I'd been having and then injuring myself on the job, I decided I had had enough. I submitted my papers and filed for a disability pension. I never returned there again, not even to clean out my locker. I thought, "If I get a pension, great; if I don't, I still won't return. That's it for me; I'm finished with them all."

Shortly thereafter and acquiring an attorney to plead my case, this fellow (my co-worker) passed away. I managed to attend his wake even though I was nervously shaken. Of course at that time I didn't know anything about endorsing myself, but I was glad I went.

It took approximately two years to finally retire. I had always thought that the day I eventually received the news of my retirement would be a happy and glorious one. And then in May 1989, my son John came with me to attend a hearing in Manhattan before the New York City Pension Board. My attorney had a few other clients he was to represent beside me. When it came time for my case to be heard, my attorney went in first and I was called in a few moments later. I was asked just a few questions and then told to wait outside until my attorney would come out to speak to me of the results. When he did, he first mentioned to me to please not get too excited when he gave me the news on whether I won or not. He didn't want the other clients of his to witness any overreaction of joyfulness that would make them even more nervous than they were already. When he gave me the good news that we won, I was elated. It was finally all over with. I thanked him and his law firm for all their help. What struck me as odd was when my son and I left the area and could now show all the emotion I wanted to, I just didn't do it. I was happy and it all felt good but why wasn't I bursting with joy? I just couldn't understand why.

I believe the emotion I was feeling was somewhat in the area of "defeat after victory" as Recovery would call it. The two years waiting to get out took its toll. I never went back to the job site, nor wanted to see, talk with or hear from anyone I had worked with. The more I withdrew from the things that bothered me, the more I feared them. I would go to bed at night and end up dreaming I was back at work. Even in the dream I would ask myself, "What am I doing here? I'm retired and receiving a pension and yet they still allow me to come in? Am I being paid a salary or just doing this on my own? But why am I doing this? I didn't like the job, so why do I keep coming in? Then again, why are they allowing me to come in to work? The dreams and the people in them seem so real. Maybe it is real and all the other stuff is a dream." The angrier I would get at having these dreams, the more I would have them. It was only later on, when I joined Recovery Inc. self-help, that I began to discover that what I was doing was only making me worse. Here's a phrase I picked up from Dr. Low's Method: "Hallucinations, delusions and dreams have the highest degree of reality, and that if a thing looks real it is almost certain to be nothing but imagined." ("Selections From Dr. Low's Works," p. 57)

One of the most important words to learn about in Recovery is the word DANGER. Dr. Abraham Low couldn't emphasize this word enough. Even in his writings he had it spelled with capital letters. What I found out was that I was attaching danger to my thoughts, dreams and symptoms and if I kept doing that it would only make the situation worse than it was. As soon as I realized it, I started to reverse the course. It made so much sense. So simple, yet so many people fell into this trap so easily like I did. When I would go to bed at night, I would now apply logic to my thoughts and fears. I would tell myself not to attach danger to my dreams because, simply, it was a dream and not real. I would say, "So what if I have one of those dreams? Let it come because I'm not going to fear it. It means nothing other than maybe feeling a little discomfort, that's all." The more I practiced Dr. Low's Method, the better I slept and the dreams died down a lot. If now and then I had one of those dreams, I would say, "So what of it?," and write it off as just a little distressing, but not DANGEROUS.

# CHAPTER 2

# DEALING WITH FAMILY STRESS

During my two-year period while waiting, hoping and praying to finally retire from my job, there were other situations I had been dealing with that I believe may have worn on me to the point of having a nervous breakdown. In 1987 my mother was very ill. She, my father and my sister, Maryann, were living in a house in Staten Island. Because my sister was still working at the time, as was my brother Paul, who also lived in Staten Island, I spent more and more of my time traveling there to take care of both of them. Anyone who's ever had to help take care of a loved one knows quite well what I'm talking about. It was one thing to clean and bathe my father at times who, of course, was a male; it was another, doing it for my mother. As her health declined she was taken to a hospital. While visiting her one day by myself and speaking to her, she took a turn for the worst and was transferred to ICU. A breathing apparatus was placed on her among other tubes and wires. She was barely conscious and shortly after, passed away. I felt both sad and guilty: guilty for being the last one in the family to talk with her, feeling the privilege should have gone to my father or my sister or brother, since I was the youngest. It sounds silly, but I think that way sometimes. You spend your life thinking about the day when your mother or father will die to the point of saying to yourself, "Stop, enough," and go on to think of something else. At times it can be difficult but you eventually do it. My mother's passing was our first experience with someone dying who is about as close to oneself as you can get. Death is something we all don't want to think of, but we learn as we get older, it isn't always the worst thing. My mother Sarah, or Sally, as friends and relatives would call her, was suffering for an entirely long time. With all her suffering and inability to function, she prayed to the Lord to take her because she could no longer take care of herself, let alone all the people she had taken care of all her life. She was now to finally rest in peace. After the funeral and returning home to retire for the night, I laid in bed and thought of my mother and what a wonderful life we all shared with her. She was a special person, a very loving and caring person to us all. We were all going to miss her, especially my father, as we were soon to find out.

In the months following my mother's death, my father's mental state was changing. Every so often Pop would start asking where my mother was. My sister Maryann would hear this more often than my brother and me, since she lived there with him. However, we would hear it also when we were with him. We would remind him that Momma passed away. He would talk about people being in the house when they weren't. We would have to explain to him that there wasn't anyone else in the house except us. Pop, hearing us explain that, would sometimes say, "Oh, okay;" other times he would say, "I hear them in the basement" or "They're upstairs. When are they going to be finished working?" Again, we would try to explain to him that no one was there. Sometimes it would work; sometimes, it didn't. If it didn't work, we would simply say, "They went home for the day" or "they finished the job." There were periods when he needed round-the-clock attention. My sister and brother were still working at the time; however, I wasn't, because my Workers' Compensation disability case was still pending. Since I had the time, I would travel out to Staten Island Mondays to Fridays. I had to arrive there early enough so my sister would be able to leave to get to her job at 9 AM in Manhattan and then remain there until she came home after 6 PM.

I would do various things such as take Pop out for a ride around, do some shopping, or get a haircut. At home I would give him a shower, cook meals, watch TV, do a little work, have a nap and have some nice conversations. I would also have him take his medication on time and bring him to the doctor or the clinic at the hospital. Pop was in his mid-eighties with failing health physically and a bit mentally, dealing with reality and unreality. A couple of times he had to be hospitalized. Amongst my sister, brother and me we devised a schedule where we were able to visit Pop at different times of the day. One day I happened to be in Staten Island and I went to my sister's house to ask if I could see Pop at the hospital at that time when she would normally be going to see him herself. She was fine with that.

I happened to be there around lunch time. When the food arrived he was propped up with the tray placed in front of him. I began to feed him when, to my surprise, he just stopped moving while I was about to place a portion of food into his mouth. There was still no movement at all. I was frozen and then the thought hit me: "Oh God, is he alive, dead? Oh my God." I was touching him and saying, "Pop, Pop, are you alright, can you talk?" There was no response. "I'd better run outside the room and get someone in here quickly to help him." Then another thought: "Maybe not, he's at peace now. Revive him just so he can continue to live in misery?" And then another thought, "No, don't play God. Get out there fast." These thoughts flashed by me in a matter of a few seconds. I ran out and summoned for help. Doctors and nurses immediately ran into the room. I was told to wait outside. Several minutes passed when one of the doctors approached me and said, "I'm sorry, your father passed away." At that moment, I did not know what to think or feel. Why was I not crying? I thought, "My father just died and I'm not crying, why?" I remember a lady patient in a room across from my father's room was so nice in consoling me. I felt a bit ashamed for not crying and a little cheapish for having been consoled.

My father was albino, his hair all white, with pink eyes. At his old job as a street mechanic digging ditches and fixing gas pipes, he was known as "Whitey" to his fellow workers. His real name was Alphonse, but nobody called him that. On his side of the family he was known as Fonsie; on my mother's side he was called Al. It didn't matter to him what he was called, as long as they didn't call him late for supper. He loved to eat and enjoy a good meal with a nice glass of wine and he never refused seconds. He was a quiet guy who never complained. Maybe another reason I didn't cry was because he died eating. Bravo Pop!

I remember as a kid and even in my adult life thinking about my mother and father dying one day. It would pain me no end. It was unimaginable and I would have to push myself to stop thinking about it. I think among my sister, brother and me, I felt I was with Pop most of the time. I liked being with him and working with him whether it was something around the house or helping someone else. I think the reason I couldn't cry was because he was at peace. It was okay, he could be with Momma. No more asking where she was or what happened to her. It would all be real again, and without the pain and suffering they both endured.

Thinking back over the years and of my involvement with my mother and father and, for that matter, my mother in-law, I found it quite ironic for me to be in such a critical position of facing life and death. It was me alone with my mother when she took a turn for the worst. It was the last coherent conversation my mother was to have and it just happened to be with me. Then 15 months later, there I was by myself feeding my father when he passed away. And a few years before my mother's death, there was my mother in-law, who had been living with us. She had cancer and was not expected to live much longer. She chose to continue staying at our house in our middle bedroom upstairs until she was to pass away. When she reached the point where she was unable to help herself, my wife and I would assist her. When she needed to go to the bathroom, I would have to lift and carry her into the bathroom and sit her down. I would leave her and then return when she had finished and take her back to her bedroom. One day I went upstairs into the bedroom to check on her. When I didn't see any movement at all I thought, "Is she gone?" I felt she wasn't breathing, but how could I tell for sure? I got a mirror and placed it in front of her mouth. I did this a few times and when I didn't see any vapor on the mirror I knew she had passed away.

I never really thought of myself as being the only one who would be there to witness a very sad and tragic event. When my father passed away I returned to my sister's house. I had to tell her the sad news and knew it wasn't going to be easy. She broke down crying and we held one another. A couple of moments passed and she began saying some things like, "I should have gone there, why didn't I go? It was my turn to go and see him." All the while I started feeling as though I deprived her of seeing Pop alive for the last time. "Maybe she's upset with herself because, had she gone, maybe Pop would have still been alive." In any case, it was a very emotional moment. One thing I know is, my sister would never do or say anything to intentionally hurt me.

At both my mother's and father's wakes, many friends and relatives came to pay their respects. There were also people my brother and sister knew from their jobs. I was constantly being introduced to all those people. However, there was never an opportunity for me to introduce any friends of mine or fellow workers from my former job. I knew why since the day I was eligible for Workers' Compensation, I never returned to my workplace, not even to clean out my locker. I didn't want to see any of my fellow workers, particularly my foreman. I wasn't comfortable with them, which was a big reason why I wished to leave in the first place. Seeing all the people my sister and brother knew from their jobs, especially my brother Paul, made me uncomfortable. Paul worked for the New York City Police Department as a Sergeant. Not only were they there to pay their respects, they were there to lead the procession. It was very nice and I respected it, though it made me feel even less than I was already feeling. I was dealing with self-pity and, as I learned later in Recovery, it was not good to dwell in self-pity, because it would only add to depression.

On the phone with my sister one day, talking about what I was going through mentally, I told her that I'd been having panic attacks and it seemed everything was bothering me. I was developing fears of doing this or that, and not wanting to go anywhere, meet people or attend social events. I feared that just going to church would cause me to have a full-blown panic attack and everyone there would see me in distress. I knew my sister was feeling badly for me and wanted to help. She reminded me, "Anthony, you were in the Army and you were stationed in Germany and you made it through all that." I remember replying to her, "I know, but that was then and this is now." It was hard to explain to anyone unless he had been in my shoes. After my sister's call, I would think back on some of the things I did in life. I wasn't an extravagant kind of person; I just did things most people would do in life. But now, just doing those simple everyday things was becoming monumental to me. I figured it was all occurring due to all of the stress I had dealt with trying to leave my job, which I eventually did. However, I must have paid the price for retiring on disability. I had hired a lawyer and it took almost two years to finally leave. I thought once I retired I would feel a tremendous amount of weight lifted off my shoulders. Some was lifted but a lot remained. I didn't feel proud of myself for fighting to retire and scoring that victory, which to me felt like an empty victory for the way I left. This was not the way I thought I would retire, although I did so because of back and neck injuries. But I knew it was more so because of all the mental stress I had been dealing with. I always envisioned my retirement would be like most people's. You have a party with friends, fellow workers and family and probably receive a watch. Well, I did have a dinner with my family and was given a watch, but it was still not the same. Yes, I got out but my pride took a hit.

 Reviewing my life at times became somewhat of a regular routine. Thinking of my talk with my sister and her mentioning my Army days made me think of how I had gotten through all that. It wasn't a big deal being in the Army and overseas; it was because of me and my quirks. I grew up on the shy side, although I always liked doing things that were physical, such as playing ball, riding a bike, running, making club houses and climbing fences and trees. However, when it came to being with relatives and at social events, I was quite shy. I remember hearing a lot, "Anthony, say something, you're so quiet, somebody got your tongue? Don't be shy" (like I wanted to be). One thing that bothered me immensely was being embarrassed and that I dreaded. I always felt I had to have my privacy. In junior high school after gym class I always refused to shower because I had to be naked alongside the other kids. That wasn't for me. If there had been private showers, that would have been different. So, because I refused, when I received my report card, I would get a very low grade. I was angry since I was good in gym and felt I should be graded on my athletic ability and not because I refused to take a shower. Using public bathrooms was another no-no for me. To urinate with someone right alongside me was next to impossible. I would stand there and just observe other men doing their thing and leaving with no trouble. And there I was, still squeezing, praying and cursing to myself at the same time. Sometimes I would just leave and hold it in. And that was awful!

One of my worst experiences was in May of 1960, when my brother, Paul, and I had to go to Whitehall Street in Manhattan to take our physical upon entering the US Army. Things were done around that time somewhat on the raw side, without any sensitivity training. We were all told to take our clothes off and to stop at each station to be examined. We were like a herd of cattle being marched around. At one of the stations we had to stand around a large round urinal and urinate in a jar. Simple, right? Not for me, though. There I was, trying to urinate with all these guys around a big tube. It didn't matter if I hadn't urinated for many hours: my muscles would become so tense they would refuse to let even the smallest amount of urine to pass. I was still standing there with this empty jar in my hand wincing and watching the other men finishing and leaving and more joining in. As my brother continued on to the next station he was looking back at me, saying, "Come on Ant, just a little will do, come on." The examiner working this station kept urging, "You could just squeeze a little out, that's all I need." I'm watching all these other guys who had no problem at all and I'm envying them. They even peed after the jar was full. I thought that maybe I could get some of their urine when the examiner wasn't looking. I was finally able to squeeze a few drops out and gave it to the examiner. At the next station I turned back to see what he was doing. There he was tilting the jar to get what little I had in the corner, so he could siphon it into his vial. Talk about embarrassing moments!

Reminiscing on that event has become a humorous ritual with the two of us. But it wasn't just what happened to me. As we continued reporting to each station an examiner told my brother to finish up there and then report to a particular office. Well, my brother did just that. So, there he was sitting with his legs folded waiting for the examiner to turn to him and tell him why he was there. As the examiner turned and faced my brother, he saw that he was still undressed. Startled to see him still naked, he quickly jumped up and told him to get the hell out of the office and go back and put on his clothes and get the hell back there. Thank God it wasn't me! That was one day we will never forget.

# CHAPTER 3

# DISCOVERING RECOVERY AND HAWAII VACATION

My first time attending a Recovery meeting was a bit of an adventure. My cousin, Rose, had called me earlier in the day and asked if I would be going to the meeting that night. She had called me a week earlier when she heard from another cousin of mine, Amelia, that I was having panic attacks. I told Rose, "Well, I'm thinking about it." She insisted that I go because it would help and wanted to meet me there. When I told her that my wife, Mary, said she would go there with me so Rose wouldn't have to, she simply replied, "I'll see you there." When my wife and I arrived, there must have been over thirty people there. I looked for Rose and sure enough, there she was. We waved and sat in the back. Looking around, I was wondering about the people who were there. These were people with mental problems. Would I be seeing any strange behavior? I saw a couple of people who stood out a bit but then again maybe it was me just thinking too much that it was strange how the meeting was being conducted. Someone would give an example of something that worked him up. The members would then raise their hands and be called on by the Group Leader to speak. What they would say sounded odd. It was not what you would think of hearing from an average person. As the meeting transpired, I realized it must have been something they learned there because other members were using similar language. These slogans were referred to as "spottings." They came from reading a book called "Mental Health Through Will-Training," one of several written by neuropsychiatrist Dr. Abraham A. Low, the founder of Recovery Inc. and the originator of the Recovery Method. The meeting was structured in a manner such that no one would speak over someone else. Everything was done in an orderly fashion so the members could get the maximum benefits of learning the Recovery Method which would help them when put into practice in everyday life. At the conclusion of the meeting, the Mutual Aid portion, I spoke with the Group Leader, Evelyn, asking if I could buy the book they were using, "Mental Health Through Will-Training." She was out of those but had a different book entitled, "Selections from Dr. Low's Works." I bought the book and she gave me an order form to purchase the other one. I told her I needed something now that could help me because on Monday I was leaving for Hawaii with my wife for our twenty-fifth anniversary. I was frightened about going and I needed all the help I could get. I had been fearful for some time over the thought of going to Hawaii. It was almost like having a death sentence. I know many would think, "Death sentence, that's ridiculous! Who wouldn't want to go to Hawaii?" Well, me! No way at all did I want to go. I knew my wife always looked forward to this day and so did I, but that was another time for me. I knew now that my life had changed and it was plenty scary.

When I returned home after the meeting I reflected on the day's events. I liked the meeting and thought it hopefully could be a help to me. I had been seeing a therapist and taking medication my psychiatrist prescribed. Now this, who knows? I thought of my cousin Rose and felt it was very nice and considerate of her coming out on this cold night to be by my side and comfort me. After the meeting I thanked her wholeheartedly. She reminded me not to hesitate to call if I needed any help. I thought about her when she first called me to

## AN OASIS IN THE WILDERNESS

tell me about Recovery. She had mentioned what she had been going through when she was in a similar situation. She had told me about all the doctors and therapists she had gone to, all the medication she was taking, the expense of it all. Wow, and on top of it all, she was raising three sons while all this was transpiring. I thought, that was absolutely incredible. I'll never forget what she told me about Recovery in her life. She stated, "Of all the doctors, therapists, medication, etc. it was Recovery Inc. that helped me the most."

I was now leaving for Hawaii. My wife and I had to get up really early, something like 3 AM. This whole thing of preparing to go was now happening. It was as though I was in some kind of a bad dream, dark out and feeling like we were the only ones awake while the rest of the world was still sleeping. I was telling myself to just take one step at a time. We made it to the airport, checked our bags in and were then waiting to board the plane. That was the next step. We were now seated and located in the center aisle. I was not too crazy about that but with the plane looking so big it wasn't too bad. I had with me the book I bought Friday night at the only Recovery meeting I had attended so far. I was hesitant to open it then because it would only keep my mind on having a panic attack. There were two things I could do if my anxiety rose. One was to read the book, the other to go to the bathroom. The bathroom would be my safe haven. I looked at it as though it was my own place, "my home," where no one could see me. It was reassuring just to keep that in mind. I was a bit tense but other than that, I was okay. I thought it ironic that when my wife dozed off and later woke up feeling a bit nervous and shaky, she immediately took off to the bathroom. Returning to her seat, she said to me, "It felt like I was having a panic attack and that's why I went to the bathroom so I could throw some water on my face." She had something to drink and was now feeling a little better. I then told her, "You're having a panic attack, and I'm not, what's going on here?"

The first night there was probably one of the worst nights I ever had. While my wife slept I was wide awake trying to sleep. We were in Waikiki and I could hear Hawaiian music softly playing continuously outside the hotel. I hated it and wished it would stop. I think between my anxiety and jet lag, I felt as though the whole world was coming down on me. I kept thinking, "I have to get some sleep. We have to get up early and join everybody from the tour at breakfast and listen to the tour guide explain what our itinerary will be. I'm not going to be in any position to understand what they are going to say. My wife doesn't hear very well and she is going to depend on me hearing them." The music continued to play and I kept on hating it more and more. It kept reminding me that "I'm in Hawaii, about 5,000 miles away, way too far from home. How will I handle myself sitting down with all the people from the tour and socializing? Oh God, please help me," I thought. "If I had a gun I would seriously consider using it to end the misery."

Somehow, it was soon time to get up. I told my wife how lousy I was feeling and said to her, "Please don't depend on me to listen to whatever is going to be said and remember it, because I haven't gotten any sleep and I'm much too nervous to concentrate." We dressed and went down to the dining room.

In the dining room were round tables with people from the tour. We sat down at one of these tables and joined in with the group. I was extremely nervous while trying my best to blend in with the rest of them. I could feel myself trembling and would hold my coffee cup with both my hands to steady it. I could feel myself standing out from the rest of them but I didn't know if they noticed it. As the day wore on we decided to go on the beach. After taking a dip in the water we stretched out on the sand to relax. There was Hawaiian music playing again just like it was when I was trying to sleep the prior night. I laid there for awhile till I couldn't take it any longer. I rose and told my wife I was sorry but I just couldn't manage to get myself comfortable and I thought it best for me to go back to the room and get some sleep there. The nap helped and I made it through the first couple of days.

My next concern was whether I'd be able to handle going to the Don Ho dinner show. The tour guide took us to the theater and had us wait by a special entrance to the front row seats which most people would love to get. The problem with me, of course, was my panic attacks. This was just what I didn't want. I would rather have been

## AN OASIS IN THE WILDERNESS

seated in the rear where I could exit immediately in case my anxiety peaked. Our seats were at the very front of the stage, great for anyone else, but a nightmare for me. To say "I prefer to sit at the back" was just too embarrassing. So, I grinned and bore it. To my amazement not only did I make it through the show (which I totally enjoyed), but we got to speak and have pictures taken with Don Ho himself. So what looked like an anxiety-filled evening actually turned out to be one of the best days that we spent there.

My next adventure was when we visited Pearl Harbor. It was after leaving Pearl Harbor and when I didn't expect it. We were on the bus and I assumed we were going back to the hotel. After riding for awhile I began thinking, "When are we going to get there? I don't remember it being this long a trip going there." With that thought, I started getting symptoms. My heart was racing and my breathing was difficult. I could feel a lot of head pressure and I started perspiring profusely. My racing thoughts were, "When are we going to get there, maybe I should ask the bus driver to let us off, but if I did that, how will we get back to the hotel?" By now the symptoms were gaining in intensity and then suddenly the bus pulled to the side of the road and we all got off to take a tour of a military cemetery. This time it was me running for the bathroom. When I got there I just kept throwing water on my face and finally got to relax. In spite of some awful moments and me not going out on a bus tour for one day in Maui, I consider it quite an enjoyable and interesting trip. We spent eleven days there, got to see three islands, enjoyed the food and the people immensely, and even made some friends along the way. This was one of those occasions where I would soon learn by attending Recovery meetings that this is where you should pat yourself on the back and endorse yourself for doing something you were afraid of and extremely uncomfortable doing.

After getting through with my eleven-day trip to Hawaii and endorsing myself, it was now time to immerse myself in attending the Friday night Recovery meetings at Mary Queen of Heaven Church. There were lots of people going to this meeting and I wondered how I would fit in. Many of the people there seemed to know just what to say after raising their hand and being called on by the Leader to comment. The comments (or "spottings," as they were called) seemed as though they were rehearsed. They were distinct phrases or quotes that were to be found in Dr. Low's books, particularly "Mental Health Through Will-Training," which was considered the main book. Some would even refer to it as their "mental health Bible." I wondered how well I'd be able to grasp not only what the members were saying but how well I would be able to say these slogans. If I thought there was a spotting I felt I would be able to say, should I raise my hand and, if called, would I screw it up? Well, after awhile I told myself "Go ahead and do it" and I did. Sure enough, I did screw it up but to my surprise, no one was laughing and the Leader clarified what I had said. She also added that it was normal or "average" (as I would soon learn to say) for a newcomer to not know exactly what to say and how to say it. This had a calming effect on me. I would notice periodically that other newcomers had the same experience. It just simply made sense that when someone was new to a group, he was not going to say everything correctly. What was emphasized, though, was the effort that was put into saying it, and remembering to endorse oneself for making that effort.

After a few weeks I was picking things up quite well. If I just didn't quite know how to say the spottings, I was understanding them more and more, and that was of utmost importance. When the meetings concluded, during the "mutual aid" portion I would notice a small group discussing going to the diner and they would huddle among themselves and then leave. I thought, "Oh well, this is probably a little clique that was formed and, besides, these things go on no matter where you go." The following week after parking my car I was invited to the diner with them after the meeting. I realized it wasn't a clique after all, it just happened to appear that way. That was the beginning of what became a ritual every Friday night. After awhile I acquired quite a bit of knowledge that I practiced in daily life. I was now doing better and better and my doctor took me off of medication. Soon after that I told my therapist that Recovery Inc. was helping me immensely. Like most people, my therapist did not know anything about Recovery Inc. and the Recovery Method. She was interested and I had brought Recovery literature for her to read. She was impressed, to say the least, and I no longer felt the need to keep attending sessions with my therapist as I felt, and she also knew, that Recovery was plenty enough to sustain me.

I now began to attend the Wednesday night Recovery group. The fellow that was leading, Joe Marino, had also been attending Evelyn's Friday night meeting. Sure enough, it was out to the diner once again afterward. I was making friends with many people now and some I would drive home after the meeting. Pat, who lived just down the block from me, liked riding along as I drove some of the people home. Before long, this socialization led to having Christmas parties, picnics and dining out with several couples and anyone else who wanted to go. For awhile we were even having dinner and dancing get-togethers.

I began assisting Joe for awhile until Evelyn asked if I would like to be her assistant at the Friday meeting. I was flattered but somewhat nervous knowing she had a largely-attended group with many veteran members including one fellow I felt would cause me to feel uncomfortable. When she asked me who it was, I told her, "Marty" and she told me, "Yes, Marty can be a little intimidating, but don't let it get to you; he's okay, and once you get to know him, you'll be alright." I accepted the post as her official assistant, and Marty, well, we became pretty good friends. He turned out to be a fun guy to be around.

# CHAPTER 4

# HISTORY OF THE ORIGIN OF RECOVERY

I eventually bought and read every book Dr. Low had written and one about him, his patients and the origin of Recovery Inc. entitled "My Dear Ones," written by Neil and Margaret Rau. I found this book to be very enlightening and would definitely recommend it to anyone. I enjoyed reading it twice and then decided to do so again, only then I reviewed it more thoroughly and noted the formation of Low's self-help organization using his Recovery Method.

In the early 1930s Dr. Low was asked to head the staff of the new Psychiatric Institute at the Research and Educational Hospital in Chicago, Illinois. He was placed in a position that enabled him to study numbers of human beings suffering from mental illness. It was here that Low used his inventiveness which enabled him to develop a Method of self-help. With the less disturbed patients, using the right choice of words had the power to energize their will to health. With Low's knowledge of language, he now was able to interview these patients and search for the effective words. Certain words which the patients used played a big part in why they became ill. Knowing this, Low would teach his patients how to reverse the trend by refraining from using words that would bring on symptoms, retain them and worsen the situation. He would train them to get accustomed to using phrases that would achieve just the opposite. Some of these were: "Replace an insecure thought with a secure thought," "Excuse rather than accuse," "Calm begets calm and temper begets temper," and "Humor is our best friend while temper is our worst enemy." This became an integral part of Dr. Low's Method. He insisted that his patients refrain from using extreme phrases such as: "I can't bear it," "This headache is killing me," or "I just knew I was dying." Other effective language became "lowered feelings" rather than "depression," and "crying spell" rather than "crying habit."

It was one thing to help those who were able to comprehend, but what about those others whom words could not reach? He became familiar with these tragic victims, those who were suffering the delusions and hallucinations of paranoia or who were living in the agonizing seesaw world of the manic depressive. Though many of them had squandered their life savings in extensive psychoanalysis or other forms of mental therapy, they had become progressively worse. Once admitted to the hospital, few of them ever left again until death released them. Each time Dr. Low would leave the hospital he was visibly shaken by the plight of the last ones he visited. Along with other physicians, he worked vigilantly in trying to find solutions that would hopefully help many of these unfortunate patients.

Dr. Low knew it wasn't going to be easy for his patients who were able to comprehend. It was "simple but not easy." He never promised them a magic pill. He would make it clear to them that insight alone was not enough. To be cured, it was necessary to put that insight into practice each and every day. He coupled a minimum of explanations with an authoritative order. "Do this, whether you understand or not, whether you believe or not. Substitute my diagnoses for yours. Substitute my positive belief in your ability to get well for your own negative fears." Low never believed that a patient was incurable. He would say, "There are no hopeless cases – helpless perhaps, but not hopeless."

On November 7, 1937 Dr. Low welcomed a delegation of some of his former patients. They came appealing to him to help them find some solution to the stigma which they felt was ruining their lives. The patients spoke openly of their illness and suffering. "Why should there be a distinction between people who are sick above the neck and those sick below the neck?" one patient asked. These patients knew there shouldn't be any distinction; it was society that didn't know. By the time the meeting broke up, the group had decided to form an organization headed by Dr. Low. That meeting in that small crowded room was the beginning of the nationwide organization which was later to be known as Recovery Inc.

At classes for these patients Dr. Low became aware of a phenomenon he didn't expect. None of them had a court order or had been committed to a hospital; yet they seemed to suffer more keenly from the sense of stigma than the committed patients. Why? It was discovered that just because they looked well and doctors said they were well, the symptoms they were getting were not just a case of nerves. Low felt, "If it were just nerves or imaginary aches and pains, then why didn't they just snap out of it?" Far in advance of his time, Dr. Low became aware that the symptoms of the psychoneurotic, like those of the mental patient, had psychological bases also. It sprang from an inborn weakness of the nervous system. It was this faulty system that caused distressing symptoms. They were the same symptoms experienced by everyone; the difference lay only in degree. They were so intense; it filled the patient with terror. Symptoms fed upon symptoms. Relatives and friends were prone to interpret the patients' very real suffering as laziness and a fundamental lack of character, which contributed to their agony by filling them with self-loathing.

Dr. Low found a way to bring both the psychoneurotics and the mental patients together at Recovery meetings. It wasn't going to be easy. Psychoneurotic patients feared even coming in contact with former mental patients. Dr. Low realized that by conquering this fear, they could eliminate their main source of tension: the fear of the permanent handicap. The philosophy was simple: "If you want to be cured, do the things you fear to do."

Annette Brocken, a former teacher and patient, was recruited by Low to attend classes and act as ambassador for Recovery. After several meetings additional members were recruited. It was the first group devoted to self-help to be established for nervous patients who had never suffered a breakdown or been hospitalized.

With World War II ensuing, Dr. Low applied to serve his country. Because of this, Annette asked him to teach the group how to study and learn so they would have something to use after he'd gone. "Impossible," Low told her. "You have to have supervision from a psychiatrist." On one memorable afternoon Dr. Low had phoned to say he was going to be delayed for about 45 minutes. Annette thought of what she could do till he got there. When the meeting began, she and other panel members discussed problems they had, the stigma and the self-help tools they had been learning. As they were carrying on with the meeting Dr. Low arrived. Rather than stepping in and taking over, he was intrigued by how well it was going. As Annette looked at him gratefully, she was ready to turn the floor over to him. He waved her aside with a gleam in his eyes and an eagerness in his voice. "No, no," he told her. "I want you to go on." As the group continued, Low listened intently. He never expected to see his patients proving they could help themselves and each other without the strict supervision of a psychiatrist. The proof was there right before his eyes.

As time went by Dr. Low realized how easy it was for the members to stray from the Recovery techniques and Method. If he was there it would be fine; if he wasn't, then what? With that in mind he inaugurated a preliminary ready of various passages of his works. They contained all the necessary techniques and by reading them the patients would be constantly indoctrinated in the true Recovery Method. Another rule Low formulated was prohibiting patients from diagnosing their ills and the ills of others and giving medical advice. Another important initiative was the five-minute phone call: five minutes for the patient to give just the bare facts to a member and for the example taker to give some words of encouragement. Going on and on with an endless tale of woe would only encourage more complaining, and thus not help the patient.

Other meetings were now being added through Cook County. Patients who had received adequate training were being assigned to lead them. All this would not have been possible had Dr. Low not been late for that one afternoon meeting. From these groups, Low compiled additional material and wrote our textbook, "Mental Health Through Will-Training."

Fortunately for Recovery, Dr. Low's application for a commission in the Medical Corp. was rejected because of his age and foreign birth. He was now free to develop the association along the new lines.

Dr. Low dealt mainly with trivialities of daily life because it was these mundane events that his patients couldn't handle. Some of his teachings dealt with "moving the muscles" when the body felt leaden with mental fatigue, making up the mind when it was torn by indecision, forcing oneself to do the things one feared to do when that thing did not represent a realistic danger. Sometimes the topic was his patients' tendency to question their bodily functions, "stepping in and taking over," as he described the process. Low would point out that the organs were designed by nature to fulfill several functions and that if left alone they would carry on very well. "Trust the power of nature within you to bring about the balance in your life," he would urge. "The body left to itself, is self-healing. You don't know how to digest an egg. Nobody knows. But your stomach does. If you leave it alone it will do it for you."

Sometimes his subject was tenseness – two kinds of tenseness, he would tell them, one stimulating and the other frustrating. The negative emotions such as envy, jealousy, hatred and self-pity poured frustrating tenseness through the nervous system. When this happened on a sustained basis, and if the nervous system was weak, all kinds of symptoms would crop up such as phobias, compulsions, obsessions, depression, anxiety and many more. But no matter how many and varied the symptoms might be, they all sprang from the one source of frustrating tenseness, and were the result of an imbalance in the system caused by tenseness. To cure this imbalance and build up nervous resistance, he explained, his patients should grow chilly to the negative emotions when they were seized with them, refuse to give them the dignity of their attention, refuse to cater to temper. He had a ready answer for these patients, who complained that holding back anger would turn them into dishrags. "Oh, no, on the contrary, you'd have self-approval," he would reply. "It takes real courage to stop temper short, much more than to give way to it. That's easy. A dog can do that."

Alternatively, he told them, if they were seized with love or joy or any of the positive emotions, they should warm to them, keep them as long as they could, for they brought relaxation which allowed nervous resistance to build. But he also voiced a word of warning against too much of a good thing. The intoxication of joy, for instance, could create an imbalance.

Low went beyond the popular school of "positive thinking" with his "constructive thinking" technique as epitomized in the Method. And so it was natural for him to provide his patients with a tool for handling their excesses of euphoria as well as their depression. They were to tell themselves, "Enjoy this moment but remember your mood is only a partial view of life. You will eventually come down from it and have to deal again with frustrations and disappointments." He would have much preferred for them to be content with less dynamic moods. "Why won't you settle for something just this side of happiness?" he would ask them almost plaintively. "Be satisfied with peace and contentment." Sometimes he spoke of gossip. Gossip, he pointed out, was indulged in because it relieved tension and boredom. But the stimulation it brought was harmful to the nervous system because it created frustrating tension. This kind of stimulus, in Recovery language, was labeled "undesirable stimulation," and it was to be avoided. Often his topic would concern the necessity of relinquishing the sense of self-importance because, as he told his patients, it was their fear that this self-importance was being threatened which caused them to panic in many trivial situations. The cure he advocated was simply an attitude of detachment toward self. "The more indifferent you are to a thing," he explained, "the less you can be insulted, or scared by it. If I am insulted, then I have a feeling of having lost my reputation. You cannot have fear if you are indifferent to the thing you are scared by... Use your sense of humor. But you cannot use your sense of humor unless you are relatively detached. This means detached from fear and insensible to insults. The more detached you become, the less can you be insulted." Over and over he would tell them, "Humor is your best friend, temper your worst enemy. Cultivate the inner smile and use it on your own foibles and shortcomings." He described the inner smile, in effect, the quiet realization and acceptance of one's own averageness.

Hopefulness was the keynote. Only a man as keenly aware as he was of the great power of words to injure in a world of increasing mass media would have spoken out so strongly against the kind of crusades being waged for various health causes by well-meaning organizations."There are too many efforts made today to strike fear in the population, to constantly warn them of danger without any visible use and perhaps, let me tell you, without any visible advantage," he said in one of his talks. "To me there is nothing advantageous in these associations that scare the population systematically. There is an organized systematic effort all over to scare you, and I have to talk to you about it because it scares particularly my patients. Patients under no circumstances should be scared, even if you think you do them good. The end does not sanction the means."

In the 1940s Recovery articles were circulating into other cities around the United States. There were more and more inquiries from people who wanted to start a meeting in their own town. People were being trained and were able to pass it on so others could open groups.

It was November of 1950 when the first copies of "Mental Health Through Will-Training" arrived at Recovery headquarters. The book was alive with examples and discussions of long-time Recovery members. They were all there, three-dimensional beings together with their lively doctor, dealing with the trivialities of everyday life. In it were condensed all the rules, techniques and insights, the quintessence of that extraordinary partnership over the years between doctor and patients – an enriching and ennobling philosophy of life applicable to everyone.

In the following years Dr. Low's patients would ask him anxiously what would become of them if anything were to happen to him. His reply was always the same. "It's all in the book. Read the book."

In St. Louis it was a Jesuit priest, Rev. Edward Dowling, a gentle man severely crippled with arthritis, who was responsible for Recovery. When he heard about it he went to Chicago to investigate it. After a brief training period, he returned to St. Louis and opened a meeting to the public at the Jesuit publishing house. This was an innovation in Recovery practice because up until then, group meetings were being held in the shelter of private homes where members were shielded from stigmatizing experiences with the public. Some were carrying this farce of concealment too far by equipping themselves with playing cards whenever a neighbor dropped in unexpectedly. Father Dowling felt it was going beneath human dignity so he provided a pattern which was presently to be adopted by the Recovery headquarters in Chicago. Home groups were now to take place at facilities such as schools, churches, synagogues and other similar public places. Recovery could now function as a free health service open to all.

Dr. Low began restructuring the organization by allowing laymen to administer it entirely. Because they were not professionals, he had to organize and set up a format that would prevent leaders and other members of the group from intellectualizing. He now presented it to them – his unique example-framework with its four-step format. From then on, streamlined examples following this format were to take the place of the loose discussion. Each example was to be followed by "spotting" from the group using only Recovery terminology. The example steps run as follows:

> Step 1: Describe the event which is to be reported as a panel example, mentioning the various things that were said and done, the persons involved, the time and then the temperamental reaction.

> Step 2: Describe the symptoms and the discomfort the member experienced.

Step 3: Describe the Recovery spotting and practice.

Step 4: Describe what would have happened before Recovery training.

Like the expressions which made up the Recovery tools, the example with its four steps looked deceptively simple. Few, perhaps, would realize how much work went into the shaping of it. Each one of the steps was carefully designed to point out "temper"– always the root cause of the patients' illness, Dr. Low had found. The new format would require a more thorough training of leaders, and Dr. Low realized the necessity of schooling one of the Recovery members to handle this delicate work and later to conduct panel demonstrations for state hospitals.

Phil Crane, a former patient and knowledgeable and dedicated member of Recovery, was chosen by Dr. Low. Also chosen to assist Phil was Ann Landis, another former patient and dedicated member. By 1952, with the final development of his self-help panel, Dr. Low himself ruled out sex, politics and religion as topic matter for examples. This rule has been followed ever since, though, naturally, members could discuss anything freely in the private conversations that took place during the mutual aid period with which every Recovery meeting closes.

Along with taped recordings of Dr. Low's lectures, "Mental Health Through Will-Training" was already proving such a success that it had long since paid for its initial outlay. People from all over the country were writing in for it, and it had gone into its third edition. The book sales were indicative of the new groups that were springing up everywhere. But in no place was the growth more phenomenal than in Michigan, due in part to Treasure Rice, another devoted and former patient of Dr. Low. With the strong growth in Michigan, it was decided that Phil Crane would travel there and have a training conference. Treasure Rice was notified and she, in turn, notified all of her leaders to gather together to receive all of this valuable training that was so sorely needed in achieving maximum effectiveness in conducting Recovery meetings. This was the first Area Leaders' Training Conference, one of many to eventually be held all over the country.

Soon Dr. Low was to travel to Detroit, Michigan to meet with the Mental Health Commission. But seeing them wasn't Dr. Low's only purpose. The Michigan clergymen had become so enthusiastic about Recovery that they were organizing a public forum to bring it to the attention of numbers of people, and he wanted to discuss this project with them in person. Even more important, he was eager to meet with the Michigan Recovery leaders. The meeting with the Commission was quickly dissipated. The discussion was polite, but it was soon made plain to Dr. Low that Recovery would not be welcome in Michigan's state hospitals.

His conference with the clergy was far more fruitful. But as he had expected, it was his meetings with the Michigan Recovery leaders that were the highlight of the day. All his affection and whimsy for these "patients" of his, most of whom he had never seen before, became apparent as he addressed them. "I want the members in your group to look to you as the leaders, and I want you, the leaders, to look to Treasure. Treasure will look to me as her leader." He paused and then added, smiling, "Never mind to whom I look."

He spoke to them as always, on a topic of their own choosing: "waiting" – the wait for the longed-for cure and the patience it required, one of the hardest and yet most necessary principles of Recovery to grasp. During the course of that classic talk, he emphasized the importance of self-endorsement, because he'd found it so often neglected by his patients. "This is central to Recovery," he told them. "So why won't you endorse yourselves? Even God endorsed Himself. Do you remember when He said, 'Let there be light,' and then there was? And after each one of those statements the Bible says, 'And He saw that it was good.'"

Afterwards, a professor of history at a Jewish college in Detroit pressed a small manual into his hands. It was an aid that would help Recovery members to study the book, he said. Dr. Low inspected the carefully prepared manual. He knew from its thoroughness that the man must have worked long, hard hours to compile it and he praised it highly. Then firmly he shook his head. "No," he said. "It's a very fine work, but I don't want anything like this. I want my patients to get it out of the book for themselves." He never approved of aids in the use of the Method. This book was to be pored over, thumbed through, read and reread. There was no facile way to obtain a thorough training.

Others far less learned than the professor crowded around. Some asked for advice on pressing problems, but most were eager just to express their heartfelt gratitude to him. "How could people profess so much love for a man whom they scarcely knew?" he asked himself, visibly shaken.

Later, from the depths of an overpowering emotion, he answered that question in his letter to Treasure: ". . . I was simply overwhelmed with their [the patients'] enthusiasm which was undoubtedly spontaneous. It was, of course, a revelation to me of something that, in physics, is called distant action. If men and women can display deep feelings towards a person whom they hardly know concretely, that cannot be the results of mere magnetism, certainly not of literary tricks and oratorical skills; it is simply the results of feelings touched and responding. From the beginning to the end, my contact with the patients was a running display of a profound attachment in which soul speaks to soul. If that is the basis on which Recovery is resting, there can be no doubt that a vital and lasting value was bequeathed to those suffering minds. I have felt it, but now I know it."

At headquarters he told them simply, "It can go on its own without me. I saw it in Detroit. Now we can start to expand – expand the Michigan way – because the leaders can carry on by themselves."

Current Recovery International self-help group meetings have extended to include many countries throughout the world. It has broadened its teaching by reaching out to colleges and schools and to those incarcerated at correctional facilities. It has also advanced into the technological areas as well, by conducting group meetings by phone and online.

# CHAPTER 5

# TAKING ON LOCAL RECOVERY RESPONSIBILITIES AND THE CHICAGO TOUR

Over time, I became more and more involved with the Recovery organization. When Evelyn's Friday night group (which was largely attended) became even more attended, I decided to ask the pastor at St. Bernard Catholic Church (which was my parish church) if we could set up a new group there. For some time, it seemed improbable, but after showing him a tape of Father Bernie Shannon (who became a priest because of attending Recovery Meetings) we were given permission to hold a weekly meeting there on Tuesday evenings. I now had my own group although I asked my good friend Lynn if she wanted to lead it since she was in the same parish as me, was in Recovery about two years longer than me, and was very capable of leading a meeting. "Don't be silly," she told me. "It was your idea and you did most of the leg work. You do it, and I'll assist you." I led that group for a few years but gave it up when Evelyn was having difficulty finding someone to take over her Friday night meeting. She had bought a house in New Jersey and was to move there soon. Now when I asked Lynn if she would be willing to take over the Tuesday group to enable me to lead Evelyn's group, she agreed. The only sad thing was that Evelyn was leaving. She was a very good Leader and a very fine person and we would all miss her dearly.

Marion, our NYC Area Leader, asked me if I would like to be her District Leader for Brooklyn and Queens, seeing how interested I was in volunteering most of my time in the growth of our NYC Area. I accepted the role and became quite active in my duties. One of them was starting up two new groups in Brooklyn and helping with one in Queens. I would end up leading one of those meetings temporarily until I was able to find someone to take over. I now led two groups, the one on Friday night, and, now this new one that was going to be held at Our Lady of Guadalupe Catholic Church in Bensonhurst, Brooklyn, which was about a 25 to 30 minute drive from my house. I never envisioned leading the Guadalupe meeting for what turned out to be about seven years, until my good friend Alan said he would be willing to lead it in my place.

In 2001 Marion had purchased a house in New Jersey and was planning to move there soon. She asked if I would be willing to take over for her as Area Leader (AL) for New York City. I agreed and thanked her. On January 1, 2002 I became the new AL for NYC. In May of that year I traveled to Chicago to be formally interviewed for the AL job even though I had been doing it for almost six months. Since it also happened to be Recovery's sixty-fifth anniversary, I had also made plans for not only my wife, Mary; I also booked eight more members from our Area to go. I had just recently learned to operate a computer somewhat and was proud of myself for booking the trip using the internet. It was just another milestone for me; nothing major, but to me, a milestone nevertheless.

That weekend in May was something to remember. We flew out there Friday morning and arrived in the afternoon about 2 PM. I had made arrangements to rent a car so that some of those who hadn't been to headquarters or seen parts of the city that Dr. Low had frequented in his day would now be able to take them in. When we arrived half of us took the shuttle bus to the hotel, and the other half went to the car rental. When I was told we would get a full size car as an upgrade at the same price, I said we were going to ride to the hotel first to pick up Bill who would have liked to have gone with us but there wouldn't have been enough room in the midsize car. We got to the hotel and hustled around to find Bill. When we found him, we told him to check his bags in at the desk and come with us. He did and we were on our way. We now had six people crammed in the car and of course, I was the driver trying to figure out where all the instruments were on the car not to mention figuring out where these places were at the same time. This was causing me to have a bit of anxiety. I did not want to waste any time because we didn't have much time. I asked for some help with the map. Holly and David were in the front with me and offered to assist me with it. My wife was seated in the back along with the other two. Here we were trying to do the best we could with limited time to do it all. I heard someone saying, "Can we stop somewhere to get something to eat?" I said, "If we do that we are going to lose valuable time; besides, we all agreed on going to the restaurant that Dr. Low used to love going to." After several minutes and thinking our friend got the message, I hear her saying, "You know, I didn't have anything on the plane to eat and I'm hungry." "Oh," I thought, "like that was my fault?"

We finally got into the city and at headquarters were given a little tour. We saw a few other sites that we had heard about and then had dinner at Berghoff, Dr. Low's favorite restaurant. "Thank God," I thought, "We can all finally sit down and enjoy a good meal and not hear anymore complaining."

When we got back to the hotel we checked in and went to our rooms. I didn't have any time to rest because I had to get to my interview while everyone else got to relax. After the interview my wife accompanied me to return the car to the rental agency. I knew there was a hospitality room at the hotel for relaxing and having refreshments. I looked forward to that after running around all day and feeling exhausted. When we arrived at the hospitality room, there was only one fellow there who informed me that there was nothing there to drink or eat. I felt, "You got to be kidding me." I had to work extra hard that night to use my Recovery training.

# CHAPTER 6

# TAKING ON MORE RESPONSIBILITIES FROM RECOVERY INTERNATIONAL

I was again honored when I was recommended by the Executive Committee of Recovery Inc. to join the Area Leaders' Support Committee (ALSC). I was invited to join by the Committee's Chairperson, Denise Holms and, after some thoughts decided to accept.

I was given a few assignments, the main one reaching out to an area that takes in three states: Georgia, North Carolina and South Carolina. The problem there was not having an Area Leader or Team Leaders for several years. I contacted all the Group Leaders to introduce ourselves to one another and asked if they would be interested in leading their Area. When they declined, I went to ask a few assistant Group Leaders, who also declined. I realized that these people hadn't been receiving any monthly Leaders' training. I decided to call some back again, especially those whom I felt would at least give it some thought. One of the Leaders from Myrtle Beach, South Carolina asked if I would give them some kind of training. What I thought might be a good idea was to go over and review our

Leaders' Guide. Being the Area Leader in NYC, I was just about to go over the new Leaders' Guide with them at our two monthly meetings in Brooklyn and Manhattan. What I did was to take certain sections from the Guide and review each one to make sure everyone understood what was meant. I would ask as we went over each item, "Are there any questions?" If there were, we would discuss it until it was clarified and then move on to the next item. I saw it was working out pretty well and thought why not do the same with the Leaders from the Carolinas? Because I couldn't physically meet them, I emailed those who had email addresses and those that didn't, I sent out by regular mail. This went on for several months until we completed going over and understanding the new Leaders' Guide. It kept me pretty busy considering I was already leading two Leaders' meetings per month where other areas may have conducted only one. NYC had the most group meetings of all the fifty-four Areas in the US and abroad. More so, I was leading two regular weekly meetings and working on one committee while chairing another one. I have to say, though, that I was pleased with myself on the way it was all getting done. And to my surprise, Lorraine Andrews, a very charming woman, presumably a senior citizen from Georgia, had called me and said that she would be willing to accept being the new Area Leader. Here was this wonderful lady willingly to be responsible for leading a three-state area. I admired her dedication especially at a time when most people are looking to relax and lessen their responsibilities.

New Jersey was another Area that needed Area leadership; however, I was fortunate to be able to communicate much better than the Carolinas because of its proximity to NYC. They didn't get an Area Leader but some of the individual meeting Leaders were volunteering to do certain jobs without taking on titles. Incidentally, I have found that to be the norm. Most people do not care to make a commitment fearing they might get stuck with the responsibility and then not be able to find a replacement when they decided to step down. I can understand that because I've been there.

Another assignment I had was with Areas in Canada. Here,

again, I was communicating with Leaders and members there. Just the practice of me calling or emailing these folks would get them a bit more motivated to communicate more with each other in their respective Areas and even with those in other Areas. To remain stagnant breathes even more stagnancy. It was now about a year since I joined the ALSC. Denise, our chairperson, informed us that the organization would like us to travel to headquarters in Chicago in April, a month before we would be returning to attend the yearly May conference. The purpose was to review every Area within the organization to identify whatever problems there might be in those Areas. We had to determine what Areas were in need of receiving immediate help, which were just getting by, and those that seemed to be doing fine. Two Areas that we focused on were in Chicago and Utah. In Chicago we had to deal with the Area's Leadership and had to figure out what was causing group meetings to be shut down at an alarming rate. In Utah we had to deal with a group of members sending in complaints about their Area's Leadership.

While in Chicago in April, and having breakfast with the committee, Bob MacIntyre, our President, came over to my table and began telling me about the work I had been doing. He said Denise was delighted with it to the point of recommending me to take over as Chair of the committee. Here I was once again in a position of adding more leadership and more work to my already heavy schedule.

I had never been a chairperson before; however, I felt as though I would be able to handle it. It was exciting and I could now explore some ideas I had that would hopefully help our organization. The following morning I told Bob I would accept the position. I thanked him and Denise for all their support. When I returned home I thought of trying something different. The idea I had made a lot of sense to me. What if each one of us was assigned a particular region which would encompass several Areas evenly so each of us could focus just on those Areas alone? We all lived in different areas of the country which also included Canada, where Joyce Oliver (one of our committee members) lived and was assigned to that Area. If we had to travel to one of the Areas we could keep traveling expenses down

## AN OASIS IN THE WILDERNESS

to a minimum. I presented the plan to our Executive Director (ED), Kathy Garcia, who supported it and got it approved by our Board of Directors.

Denise's region was the west coast since she lived in Sacramento, California and one of her Areas was in Utah. The problem in that Area was mainly with the Area Leader (AL) and a Group Leader (GL) and some of her friends who attended her meetings. Several letters had been sent to headquarters complaining about their AL and how she continued to chastise the GL. I had read all the letters along with Denise. When our Committee was in Chicago we had reviewed and discussed some of those complaints. The thinking at that time seemed to support those who were complaining. I told Denise I would work with her because of what I had known already. We started by making some phone calls to both parties involved in the complaint. After listening to both of them we were mixed on who was at fault. With that in mind, I felt the best thing would be to contact all the other GLs in that Area and see what they had to say about their AL. When Denise and I reviewed our findings they seemed to favor support for their AL. We even received comments complimenting their AL for going the extra mile for them when they needed it the most. It was now turning out to be more in the AL's favor. I decided to make a few more calls to some I'd already spoken to maybe two or three times before. Denise and I found that almost all were kind and polite and I remember a couple of them inviting us to come there and visit with them and they would be happy to take us for a tour of their Area that was mainly in the Salt Lake City area. I thought that to be very nice of them and, who knows, maybe one day I would take them up on it. Putting everything in perspective I now felt confident in my conclusion of what had been occurring. The GL who felt she was being chastised had not been attending required monthly Leaders' meetings. Missing a few was average but in this case it was extensive. Additionally, the feud went back several years earlier when there was an Area Team in place instead of an Area Leader. The present AL was part of that Team that may have consisted of three to five Team Members. Over the years some of these Team Members would quit with no replacement. Some had left because the then-current AL was somewhat bossy. The complaining GL knew about this, but she was also not attending Leaders' meetings, arriving late at her meetings etc. These members supported their GL because she was also a friendly, hospitable person who liked to invite her friends to parties at her home quite often. Several of those group members expressed these things to me and I began to understand why there was this conflict. Even the AL stated that maybe she was a little too tough in the beginning but she said, "I thought that's the way I had to be." In conclusion, I wrote a letter to all the Leaders and group members who had in some way been involved in the conflict. Sometime thereafter, things quieted down and Denise and I felt confident that the matter was resolved. I did hear from a couple of them later on and thank God it was all positive.

Looking back from that April when we were in Chicago, it was almost a sure bet that the AL would have been found at fault, reprehended or removed as AL. We would then have had to hopefully find a replacement. Whether she was removed or not, she probably would have just resigned in any event. When you have volunteers doing these jobs, it's very easy for them to simply say, "I quit," then what? I was content with myself for looking into this matter thoroughly. Things were getting done and Areas were getting a bit livelier since our Committee was contacting them, helping out and giving them support. Areas like Nebraska, Missouri, Kansas, Kentucky, California, New Jersey and even Canada were being attended to and functioning a bit better. Our Committee became more and more of a working committee. I knew even with these achievements, we still had a long way to go. Considering we had about six to seven people on the Committee, we wanted to add a few more. I started getting some names recommended to me. I wanted to insure that any additional recommendations for our Committee would be able and qualified to do the job, and from time to time I would make sure to mention to our Committee that if they felt overworked, we could get additional assistance in getting their assignments done. What I got mainly from them was: "I'm okay, I'm fine and maybe later I could use some help," comments like that. Because those were the answers I was getting I was more selective in who I was to add to the Committee. Around this period two veteran Recovery members, Joan Nobling and Mary Gillen, were added to the paid staff. Joan had the title of Training Director and Mary as Support Director. I was delighted that Mary, a person I enjoyed talking to and being with, would now work quite a bit with me since she was involved in the support area of the organization. I looked forward to it. Our Committee had also changed its name. It was now called the Area Support Committee (ASC). The word "Leader" was dropped because we were in support of the Area mainly, and the way it was before made it sound as though it was only the Area Leader. Holly, a good Recovery friend of mine made the suggestion and I brought it to the Board of Directors' attention and it was approved.

While we (the Executive Committee, Board of Directors, Support Director and I) agreed on most issues, there were a few with which we had our differences. One involved a person being barred from attending weekly Recovery meetings. I disagreed somewhat with those officials who wanted the person barred. I felt this issue needed to be looked into more carefully, especially when it was our Committee's job to handle it and we were not informed of it until a year later. I did receive an apology and accepted it. I always felt that before anyone is barred from going to meetings, the Group Leaders and Recovery officials should go as far as necessary. After all, the meetings we have are for people dealing with mental health issues. They are attending for the same reasons we had when we first began. Some people can be a little more difficult than others. When I conducted monthly Leaders' Meetings the Leaders would discuss annoying and upsetting incidents that happened at their meetings. We would talk about how we could deal with these situations. We had a Leaders' Guide to guide us. If we couldn't find it in the Guide, we would discuss it and work on finding ways we could remedy the situation. Being from New York City I attended and led many meetings and witnessed all kinds of misbehavior but, overall, I considered them as just (in most cases) a portion of the full meeting. I would tell the Leaders on many occasions, "If you got through the meeting and felt as a whole that it was a good meeting or at least an average meeting, consider it okay and by all means, endorse yourself for all your efforts." The idea was to focus more so on the positive rather than on some of the minor irritations that happen now and then.

So now I was involved with a person who was being barred from attending Recovery meetings in Ohio. I believe Bob MacIntyre wrote the letter that officially barred him. The letter was sent out to him about a year or so before I was told about it, and the problem eased because some GLs were permitting him to attend while some others were not. What needed to be done was to get everyone in that Area organized and follow the proper protocol. A telephone conference call was set up among Mary Gillen (ASD), Bob Nies (ASC member), Natalie (AL) and me (ASC Chair). One other GL from that Area joined us on the call that probably had the strongest feelings in not having the barred person attend her meeting. After Natalie and the GL spoke, Mary, Bob and I spoke and gave our opinions. Bob and Mary both felt the barred person should remain barred from all meetings. I requested and was granted a little time to try and find a solution that would be acceptable to the GLs in that Area and the barred person. I was granted the time but I also knew I wasn't going to have much time, feeling I was in the minority.

I emailed the barred person and told him that as Chairperson of the ASC, I might be able to assist him in rectifying the situation that got him barred. I asked him to explain his side of the story because he claimed his side of the story was not taken. I told him who I was and what my role was in all this as Chairperson of the ASC. I also told him I would like to speak to him on the phone. In his email reply he stated emphatically that he would rather correspond with me by email, since he didn't want to say something over the phone that he might later regret. By email he felt he had time to review what he wrote before sending it. I replied back saying I could understand his reasoning but I felt we could use the phone sparingly to clarify some things that may have gotten misinterpreted. He wouldn't go for it. So now I had to spend hours on top of hours reading and writing emails. Writing these emails was taking a lot of time and I started to feel pressured by Mary, Kathy and Bob MacIntyre. I felt there wasn't going to be much time left for me to resolve the matter and I had both stubborn sides pressuring me. I knew if I didn't reach a solution soon, it would be taken out of my hands. I considered a compromise, as a fair decision. I had to get the barred person to go along with it and that wasn't going to be such an easy task to pull off. In his emails he would always talk about his determination to fight this thing through even if it meant taking legal action. Nevertheless, I couldn't go any further. I had to pose an ultimatum.

I set out to write what could have been my last email to him. I told him I figured out a solution that I believed would be accepted by Bob MacIntyre: for him to agree not to attend the group meeting that the GL would leave if he attended. However, he would be allowed to attend the other group meeting. I told him I felt confident this could all be worked out with all those concerned, including him as long as he accepted it. My ultimatum was: "If you don't accept, this will be my last email to you." I told him I had worked very hard to prevent him from remaining barred but couldn't go on any longer. I made it as clear to him as I could, "You don't accept, then that's the end of me." Well, unfortunately, he did not accept. About a year later, I received an email from him stating, "I'm sorry I didn't listen to you and accept your recommendation. I realized you were the only one from the Recovery organization that truly tried to help me. Thanks." I never replied.

# STRATEGIC PLANNING (GETTING RECOVERY BACK ON ITS FEET AGAIN)

When Kathy Garcia first came on board, she realized her job as Executive Director was not going to be such an easy one. The organization was losing meetings along with decreased attendance. I happened to be at headquarters in Chicago when Kathy was on the computer creating a chart of all our Areas beginning from 1990 to the present. I was there with Bob MacIntyre and I believe it was the first time I brought up the idea of creating regions within all the Areas of Recovery. As Bob and I were discussing this we met up with Kathy. She showed us the chart she was working on and asked me when I began with Recovery. I told her, "1990," and she replied, "No wonder, and that figures." She told us that chart was to see how all the Areas faired in growth. The majority of the Area meetings were significantly negative. Chicago, our home city, was down about 40%. Out of a small amount of Areas on the plus or positive side, New York City was on the plus side gaining about 40%, the highest of all the Areas. Now I knew what Kathy meant when she said, "No wonder and that figures." The compliment was satisfying but I knew it wasn't all about me. Our former AL, Marion Zukoff, along with Marion's Assistant Area Leader, Anna Feuerman and her husband and Treasurer, Artie Feuerman, had a lot to do with it. Other than the few Areas that had done well, it was sad to see such a negative chart. Now we knew for sure something had to be done to turn this organization around. The problem was, how, what and when?

Both Kathy Garcia and Bob MacIntyre felt it time to get into Areas that needed to be changed. Deep-seated items that needed to be worked on: items that would bring out controversies, especially those that delved into areas that most conservative traditional members would not like to address in fear that it might lead to diluting the standards which Dr. Low had put into place some seventy years prior. The thinking was that these standards were important and they needed to be maintained so that the patients attending the group meetings got the full benefits of them. Lowering the standards by making it easier for the patients to get by would conceivably be detrimental to their mental health. Dr. Low would say from time to time, "The Method is simple but it's not easy." He insisted that, "Merely knowing the Method is not enough, they have to go through the training." The organization's thinking started to be, "Yes, that was fine for years ago but not today." The present-day organization felt that some changes should have taken place years before to blend in more with the modern day culture. Had that been done, they felt we wouldn't be in the situation we were in then. My thoughts were that I could go along with some of that thinking but, then again, what if we were wrong and loosened up and nothing changed for the better or even got worse? Another thing: I felt what made this organization strong and effective was its uniqueness in maintaining discipline as an essential ingredient in learning and, above all, practicing the Recovery Method. I didn't fear change; I feared what those changes might be. I thought that common sense should prevail. I saw how easily Recovery people were being labeled. If we were opposed to a particular change, we were simply labeled "against change." This did not sit well with me. The people in the highest positions, mainly our Executive Director, President, Executive Committee and most members on the Board of Directors, pretty much took on that attitude.

Recovery was now set to get into many areas that would hopefully lead to new growth. Some of these areas were going to be controversial. A new committee was added called The Methods and Meeting Committee (M&M). The objective of this Committee was to review the Recovery Method and the Recovery meetings and look for ways to make any changes that would help in bringing in more people. The Committee chair was Bob MacIntyre, and both Phyllis and Marilyn, two daughters of Dr. Low, and several prominent others, were on the Committee. At times I would talk with Bob MacIntyre about interest with what they got to work on. At a Board meeting in Chicago where the new "strategic planning" was begun, Bob, to my surprise, mentioned that he decided to add me to the M&M Committee. He knew of my interest and also thought it would be a good idea to include me since I was more of a traditionalist in Recovery than the other members and that it would at least balance the Committee to make it more objective. I was elated and accepted the position. I was now going to have first-hand access to any talks and possible changes pertaining to meetings and the Method. I was also going to be working with the two Low daughters, something that I was looking forward to.

During the period of strategic planning we had to travel back and forth to Chicago to attend the sessions beside our customary times in May and November. We also began to hold conference call sessions when not in Chicago. During this period I was also appointed to be on the Board. Two days before officially being on the Board and while attending a Board meeting, an item that I was opposed to was to be brought up to a vote on whether to accept it or not. When it came time for that to be introduced I raised my hand and asked, "I would like to read a short paragraph on page 273 from the book, "My Dear Ones." It's one of the main reasons why I believe we should vote no on accepting the use of a Tool List to be used at Recovery meetings. I was granted time to speak and I was quite nervous. I began:

*Afterwards a professor of history at a Jewish college in Detroit pressed a small manual into his hands. It was an aid that would help Recovery people study the book; he said Dr. Low inspected the carefully prepared manual. He knew from its thoroughness that the man must have worked long hard hours to compile it and he praised it highly. Then firmly he shook his head. "No," he said, "it's a very fine work, but I don't want anything like this. I want my patients to get it out of the book for themselves." He never approved of aids in the use of the Method. The book was to be pored over, thumbed through, read and reread. There was no facile way to obtain a thorough training.*

When I finished, a hand went up. It was Marilyn Low Schmitt. She said, "Tony Ferrigno is correct." The members turned to look at her, surprised as I was. She went on to add, "Even my mother knew that and supported it even after his death." Now the "but" came in and killed whatever momentum there was to prevent the list from being approved. Marilyn then went on to explain why she felt it should be accepted. It was Thursday and I asked if I was officially on the Board so that I could vote. Bob, said, "No" and then added, "You will officially be on the Board Saturday." Everyone laughed including me and then I replied "Well, when it comes to me it seems I'm always a buck short and a day late." The vote would have been unanimously accepted had one Board member not voted "No." This member explained he knew his Area members would not have wanted to accept the list. I shook the member's hand and we both laughed it off. I pretty much knew it was going to pass, but I endorsed myself for speaking up. I knew a couple of members on the Board that I felt might not vote for it, particularly one who spoke to me just recently and said he didn't like it. I could understand not commenting on the subject but, voting for it, that just made me scratch my head even more.

Here's how the Tool List originated. Bob MacIntyre had asked a few members on the Leaders' Training Committee (LTC) to come up with a list of about thirty spottings and submit them to him and he, in turn, would submit them to us on the M&M Committee. When I read the spottings I knew immediately some were incorrect. They may have sounded pretty good but nevertheless they needed to be corrected or replaced. Bob MacIntyre thought they were fine enough and wanted to get them approved by the Board. I told Bob and the Committee that they should be corrected or replaced. Bob disagreed with me and felt I was making a big deal out of nothing. I told Bob they also needed to be verifiable. "Why?" he asked. I stated, "Because we represent the Recovery organization and we bear the responsibility of making sure what we print up and distribute is authentic." I continued, "Anything less would be irresponsible." I tried to explain that anyone can make up a list of spottings and many people do. I mentioned that I made up a list of hundreds of spottings and verified many of them by referencing from what book, chapter and page number they came. The outcome was to make a couple of changes, get it approved by the Board and print up a batch of them. There were no verifications or citations printed on the list. I requested to be assigned a detail of getting verification and adding citations to the list, deleting those that were unverified and replaced with those that were. I was granted permission and to my surprise, Marilyn and Phyllis volunteered to assist me. Cliff Brown from LA was added to this subcommittee because of his knowledge in these areas. The job for us was to go through three of Low's main books: "Mental Health Through Will-Training," "Selections From Dr. Low's Works" and "Manage Your Fears, Manage Your Anger." Out of the thirty spottings, I already had about half of them verified from my own list. Now, we just needed the other fifteen or so to complete the list. It was a bit of an ordeal but we managed and completed it fully, verified with citations to show their origin. The funny thing about this spotting list was that I was opposed to having one and here I was, probably the one who did the most work on it! As I said earlier, I pretty much knew that a Tool List was going to be approved. With that, I figured if we were going to have one, it had better be a good one. I was satisfied in the end. When some people would ask me, "Why would you be opposed to something like this?" I would mention what I had previously mentioned about Dr. Low not wanting aids in the training of the Recovery Method. I could see Low's point and thought it was a good one. It was sort of like the show, Jeopardy, where you get the answers first and then supply the question. Or, you're in school and the teacher asks the students questions and then supplies them with the answers. One more: the teacher wants you to write a book report and what do you do? You write what's on the inside or outside of the book jacket cover and submit it that way. I was guilty of doing that a couple of times. So, here you see what Dr. Low was telling us when he said, "I want my patients to get it out of the book for themselves." The book was to be pored over, thumbed through, read and reread. There was no facile way to obtain a thorough training.

# CHAPTER 8

# CONTROVERSIES, STONES AND SETBACK

There was increasing talk about the possibility of merging the ASC with the LTC. If not merging we were to work a little closer with each other. Arrangements were being made for the LTC to go to Orlando, Florida which also included me. I made arrangements and booked a flight. Unfortunately, I developed kidney stones. I had never had this problem before and it was coming at a bad time. My doctor was away on vacation so I was set up to see another one. When this substitute doctor examined me, he felt I needed to have the stones removed immediately. He set up an appointment for the procedure on the coming Monday and I was set to leave a day or two afterwards. As it turned out I canceled my flight to Orlando because I had a stent placed that was to remain in place for about a week. Not all the stones were removed, however. I now had to have another procedure, this time by the doctor with whom I had originally begun. Afterwards I had to journey back to Chicago feeling a bit worn down, but I managed. Over the next couple of years a lot was going on and I began to develop some nervous symptoms. They were getting progressively stronger and stronger and it started to affect all my work with Recovery. Another trip to Chicago was approaching and

I began dreading going. Being on two committees, chairing one of them, on the Board and being responsible for taking care of my Area in NYC (not to mention my own two group meetings and Leaders' meetings), I was doing it all and it began to overwhelm me to the point of making an appointment to see my doctor. My Recovery training was helping me, however, even though I was now feeling in worse shape than I had ever been.

I received a call from Bob MacIntyre one evening. He wanted to review a particular item that concerned me and the ASC. He went on to tell me that he and the Executive Committee (EC) had agreed to merge the ASC and LTC with Ruth Reynolds remaining on as the chairperson. I was to remain on this Committee but would no longer be chair. I was startled at what I was hearing. I asked him, "Why wasn't I included in this discussion? After all, I was chairing the ASC." He replied, "It was just the EC," then I said, "What about Ruth Reynolds, she was there." He said, "Yes, but she's on the EC." I told him again, "Well as chair, I still feel I should have been included." I went on to tell him that I didn't think it was a good idea to merge then and that I was not necessarily against merging; I was against it being done at that time. He told me, "It's going to be brought up at our next Board conference call meeting and then voted on when we're in Chicago next month." When we got off the phone I was quite upset. I knew our Committee was doing a very good job and I couldn't see why they didn't understand that. We were not even into a full year of working with regions and so far things had been going well. Why disrupt it now? When we had our Board conference meeting I told them to please be patient and hold off for a little while so we could make sure whether it was a good idea to merge then or later, or whether to even merge at all.

I needed to make reservations to travel to Chicago but felt I couldn't do so. The way I'd been feeling made it seem impossible to go. But what about the Board voting on the merger, my Committee etc.? It was probably the worst time not to go. I called Mary Gillen and nervously told her I was deep into symptoms and having a setback. Every time I thought about going to the conference I would feel overwhelmed with even more symptoms. I'd been using my Recovery training but it just seemed too much for me to handle. Mary pretty much understood, we were nervous patients and nervous patients understand things like this. Dr. Low warned us about setbacks when he said, "Expect them" and would go on to explain, "Expect them and don't give up on the Recovery Method. You've been there before and what you've done before, you can do again." After speaking with Mary I felt a little better. She told me, "Take care of yourself, and don't let it get to you. We'll manage and take care of things in your absence."

    Denise had gone to the conference and had told me she would call and fill me in on what was transpiring. Denise became a good friend of mine and I always appreciated when she would do things like that. Even without asking her she would do it. When I got the news that the Board voted to accept the merger, it troubled me. Why couldn't they wait, what was the big hurry? The Committee and I worked diligently unlike some other committees and all we asked for was to be a little bit patient, and we couldn't even get that. The Board would go by what the ED and the President would suggest to them. Kathy and Bob, with whom I enjoyed working and being good friends, were getting to be more and more aggressive in their actions to turn this organization around. I looked at it as simply being impatient. The actions they had been taking were already unprecedented in the almost 70-year existence of the organization. I felt Kathy and Bob and a few others were becoming more and more influential, causing them to be bold in their actions. "Change" was the big word. If you agreed with them, great; if at times you didn't, you were against change. It had become that simple. In for "change," you were with the in crowd; not for "change," you were with the out crowd. It started to feel there were no "in-betweens." It was kind of like what Dr. Low would call "the extremes." What happened to the middle of the road (average)?

    Prior to the Board voting on the merger a letter was sent out to encourage the members to vote in favor of the merger. Anyone reading this letter without knowing some of the facts would assuredly go along with it. Were they lying in the letter? I guess you can say they weren't and you would technically be correct. As Chair of the ASC I knew they weren't telling the whole story. And this is why I should have been included in the merger talks with the Executive Committee. If they wanted, they could have talked again, this time without me. I think that would have been fair. Had I been there I could have pointed out these things and objected to what they were saying or implying in the letter. Here are some of the points that were included in the letter, followed by my comments:

A.  The ASC was powerless.

Powerless? In an organization that is a non-profit and deals mainly with volunteers, that's a strong word to use. If I had to choose a word I would use "influential." We would talk to leaders and members and use our influence to have them function in accordance with the best interests and good of the Recovery organization.

B.  Tony was having a hard time finding people to be added to the Committee.

Yes, I was having a hard time finding people to add to the Committee. However, what the letter didn't include was: having a hard time finding "good, qualified people" to add to the Committee.

C.  We were overworked.

I don't know what they considered being overworked, but I do know the Committee was not being overworked. As a matter of fact, I would ask them from time to time if they had too much to do and the answer would always be "No." I would even remind them that if they did, to let me know and I would see to it that they would get some help.

D.  We had too many Areas assigned to each member.

Nobody was complaining and if someone did I wanted them to

tell me and I would lighten their load by getting them some assistance. Also, if this happened I already knew there would be a good chance some other committee members who did not have a heavy load and with very little going on at that time, would be able to assist the other committee member.

What we were doing was still in the trial stages. I did add two people to the Committee around that time. One of them went on to a higher position and became a big asset to the organization. When they came on board, I told them I wasn't going to assign them any Areas for the moment. One of them was from the west coast and a good friend of Nancy Campbell. Being a good friend of Nancy, I told her she could assist her when needed. I think we now had about eight people on the ASC.

With me in a setback and having friendships which seemed to be deteriorating day by day, I found I had to make some decisions I really didn't like; however, I had to consider my mental health. I got in touch with Kathy and explained my situation. I told her I thought it best to resign from the Board, and also as Regional Leader (a position I pretty much created) and when I mentioned resigning from the M&M Committee she told me I could stay on that one and not feel obligated to go to Chicago if things were still bothering me. So, I remained on it. I also knew I had to make changes in my own NYC Area.

The ASC and the LTC had now merged and was named the Area Support and Training Committee (ASTC). It consisted of about fourteen Regional Leaders (RL), double the amount as before. One RL who had been added was someone I knew and felt should not have been appointed RL. He had been a veteran member and was well known throughout the organization. But he didn't fit the qualifications required to be on this committee. He was simply added on by influential friends. I knew this person in the earlier days of the ALSC. He did very little work and was usually last when turning in his assignments. And when he turned them in, they were very brief. He was also someone for whom I got a group meeting in NYC which he needed so as not to become suspended as a member of the LTC. The LTC was a Committee which traveled a lot and had its expenses paid. It was one of the reasons it was a popular committee. When I told the Board of his shortcomings, it didn't seem to go anywhere. As a matter of fact, I was even called, "out of line" by the Board Chair for speaking about him.

It was about a year later when I received that email from the barred person I mentioned earlier. I had called Kathy to tell her about it since I was no longer on the Committee. When I mentioned it to her she said, "Who has that Area?" When I told her his name, she in turn replied, "Oh, he's not going to do anything." I said, "Kathy, I can't believe you said that," and I then felt vindicated. I tried to warn them but they just wouldn't listen. She also told me, "Tony, why do people volunteer to be on a committee and then don't do anything?" I replied, "I don't know, maybe it's the free traveling?" Kathy, Bob and Mary were now discovering what I had been telling them all along. Many of the RLs who were added weren't getting the job done as they had expected. I wondered if they remembered what I had said back then, "It wasn't that I had a hard time finding people to be added to the ASC; I was having a hard time finding good people to put on the ASC." What were they going to do now? Now they thought that perhaps if they paid the RLs the job would get done. The only thing was, could they afford paying them? Now they figured on hiring about four people with one of them being a manager. They proceeded with that idea and set up interviews with those applying for the jobs. I still had to deal with my setback but I was improving every day so I figured I'd better put in for the job then and hopefully feel better when or if they selected me. I applied for both the Manager and Regional Leaders jobs not knowing for sure if I would accept them. It was kind of funny when Mary interviewed me for the Manager job. I even told her that. "Hey, we worked together practically every day when I was the Chair of the ASC." She said she knew that but had to be fair. I thought, "Wouldn't I be best qualified being I was the one who started this thing with the regions and had firsthand experience from its inception?" Well, to no surprise, I didn't get either of the two jobs. It was kind of like Thomas Edison being interviewed for the first electrician job and then not getting it. Maybe I'm exaggerating a bit but it did seem a bit strange with a twist of both humor and hurt feelings thrown in. I don't know, but maybe it was best for all concerned.

Now Recovery had people on the payroll probably more than they ever had. The organization had applied for a grant which they thought they were going to get for sure but it fell through. Those that were recently hired had now been fired and RI was in fear of being bankrupt. It appeared that they were spending money before they even had it in the bank. Who was responsible for this? Questions were being raised but very few answers were being given. Our more recent Executive Director who at that time took over when Kathy Garcia sadly passed away was fired and now we had to look for a new ED. A couple of years before this unfortunate incident took place our old HQ on Dearborn Street had been sold for $1 million. Headquarters was now functioning out of an office building which they had been trying to downsize to save some money. Our name had been changed a few times after about seventy years. It went from Recovery Inc. to Recovery International. Then it went to The Abraham Low Self-Help Systems and then back to Recovery International. Each time there was a change of name, money had to be spent in changing all our literature including all local banking areas. Yearly training conferences were canceled to save money. Most things were now being done through phone conference calls. When strategic planning had been going on we set a goal of having 800 group meetings by the year 2007. With over 600 groups from around the year 2002 we had been steadily declining to less than 400 after the year 2007.

Would things have been better or worse had we done nothing? I don't know. However, what I do know is we did not succeed in our mission to "change" the status quo.

A few years ago I mailed a letter to all the Area Leaders and Team Members within the Recovery organization. I wrote about having elections for our officials. I stated my reasons and mentioned a few other things I considered worthwhile speaking about. I had asked for them to send me a reply giving their thoughts. The replies I got back were overwhelmingly in my favor.

As I was adjusting to some of the changes that were ensuing in my life, first consulting a therapist and soon after a psychiatrist who put me on medication, I once again had fallen victim to kidney stones. I was helping my son Michael with some work in his house and throughout the day I was feeling rather uncomfortable. I had progressively been feeling worse as the day went on. When I left to go home, which was going to take about an hour, the pain had gotten so much stronger. I told my wife I was going upstairs to lie down, hoping that the pain would subside. Unfortunately, when it didn't, I called an ambulance so I could get to the hospital immediately. Once I arrived, though, the doctors wouldn't administer a pain medication until they knew exactly what was causing all the pain. I was put in a wheelchair to wait. The pain was excruciating and I remember kicking the walls and saying, "Give me something please." While experiencing all this pain, a gurney was passing by with a female patient on it. When it stopped the lady saw me and said, "I know you." I looked at her and tried to figure out if I knew her. She said it again and I started talking to her. I didn't recognize her but said, "Recovery." I think she said, "Yes" and we began to talk. Well, I didn't mind for a little while but she was going on and on while at the same time I felt like screaming. As bad as I was feeling, I managed to find a little humor in it. Just think about it when you may have been in the worst kind of pain and somebody wants to have a bit of a chat with you. Maybe she helped, I don't know, but at least she made me find the humor at a time when I was at my worst.

After about an hour and a half they finally gave me a shot of morphine. It was the stones again. I was now with my third doctor and on my third procedure. This doctor used a more modern procedure and one I read about. A camera is used and when the stones are seen another instrument is inserted to grab the stones and remove them. I went about a week later to have the stent removed. That was also painful but at least this doctor performed much more quickly than the first doctor. I think I would have rather been water-boarded than go through what that first doctor had put me through. About a month or two later I went back to the doctor's office for a routine check-up. He also took a sonogram of both my left and right side just to see how everything looked. As he was doing so and saying, "Boy, these guys won't leave you alone," I was startled by what I was hearing. He now was checking the other side and detected the presence of some stones there also. I was startled again. My thoughts were racing, "When is all this going to end? How much more can I take?" I didn't know he was going to give me a sonogram. I thought, "If he had removed them why would he be checking to find them?" When he finished the examination he informed me, "They are small and they probably won't bother you." I told him about my anxiety and that I don't know how I was going to handle all this. He was now looking a little nervous himself as though he wasn't expecting to hear this from me, a grown man. On my way home my thoughts were racing as quickly as could be. I was even having thoughts of driving off the highway and hopefully into the Atlantic Ocean. When I got home my wife was in the kitchen reading the newspaper. I began to explain everything when I just lost it and slowly fell to the floor. I don't know how I made it through the day but I did. When I felt a little stronger I decided to call the doctor. I asked, "When you did the procedure you told me you got everything out. Isn't that correct? "He replied, "Yes." Then I said, "If everything was out why did you discover there was more the day I went for the sonogram?" He said, "I got out everything I could see." I'm thinking now, "Everything I could see. Everything I can see." I said, "Everything you could see, you mean if you would have seen it, you would have removed it?" He said, "Yes." I may have said something further but felt I finally got the answer. He told me, "Lay off the salt and drink plenty of water and you should be alright."

# CHAPTER 9

# THE TWILIGHT YEARS AND THE SADNESS

Leading two group meetings a week was beginning to get to me, especially seeing meetings in my Area closing down. I hated to close a meeting down and would do all I could to keep it going. With attendance on the decline, seeking out leaders became more and more difficult. If I did find someone who was willing to lead the meetings they were usually not all that qualified. With that being the case I usually ended up with two options: take a chance and hope he would at least do enough in helping people to improve and continue to attend, or close it down. Before I became Area Leader I saw us rise to 31 groups. When I was printing up meeting lists it was getting a bit difficult fitting them all on one sheet of paper, which was a problem I liked taking care of. We were somewhere down to about 19 to 20 groups. Making up meeting lists had gotten easier. But, I didn't want it to be easier. I gave up my Saturday group when my good friend Allen was willing to lead it. Allen knew he didn't have all the qualities of a leader but he did have the dedication. He would travel from one end of Brooklyn to the other, taking maybe two to three buses in getting there and back home while using a cane because of his disabilities. That's true dedication.

I reduced the amount of Leaders' meetings from two to one a month. The odd month we'd conduct in Brooklyn, the even month we'd conduct in Manhattan. My one meeting on Friday night at Mary Queen of Heaven Church was now itself losing attendance. This was the meeting I first started at in 1990. Back then it would easily have some 30 to 40 people and now it was down to just a few. It was hard dealing with these situations and at the same time trying my best to maintain my own mental health. The many things I was doing whether locally or organizationally never felt like a job. Now it became a job. When I attended my Friday night meeting, I felt I really didn't want to be there. If in about 10 or 15 minutes no one else was there yet I would begin thinking maybe no one would show up and then hoped that would happen so I could go home. And when someone walked in I'd get turned off. I would think, is this what we've come down to? People don't care if they are late or leave early, or whether they even go or not. If they don't care, why should I? I always wanted to see newcomers and was always anxious to speak with them. When the Mutual Aid portion of the meeting came up I looked forward to speaking with them. I would pour my heart out trying to help them understand so they could return, learn the Method, practice it, get better and then observe them helping others. Wow! I remember a Leader asking me at a Leaders' meeting, "How long should you stay before leaving when no one shows up?" I said, "I used to say, at least an hour, then I went to 45 minutes and then to a half hour." I then added," Now, I'm working on 15 minutes." There was some laughter.

Among some items that may have brought on my setback was my son, Michael, and his girl friend, Annette, becoming engaged to be married. He, along with his fiancée, was now making plans for the wedding. However, before making these plans they thought it a good idea for my wife and me to visit Annette's parents who live in Minnesota and where Annette grew up. They booked a five-day package deal for Annette's parents, my wife and me and themselves at a resort up north from where Annette's mom and dad lived. This was their Christmas gift to us. It was planned for the summer. We knew nothing about this trip until a little before Christmas day when we received a Christmas card from her parents, Ken and Grace. In the card they wished us happy holidays and said they looked forward to seeing us when we would come there. We didn't know we were going but now it looked as though we would have to. We weren't sure if it was a mistake until Christmas when we received the plans of the trip. In one way, we appreciated the gift but, in another way, we felt we were put in an awkward situation. We decided not to make a big issue of it and when the summer came we went. I experienced some discomfort with nervous symptoms but other than that, it turned out really well. Her parents were delightful people and down-to-earth the way we were. The rest of the family and relatives were also very nice and hospitable. The flight home was another story! The plane was sort of a compact type and I was claustrophobic, vulnerable to having panic attacks. However, everything went fine until we landed. We were waiting to get off the plane while it was at the terminal but nothing was happening and we didn't know why we weren't being let off. After about a half hour the pilot told us we had to wait for another plane's passengers to exit. He didn't say how long we had to wait and was being very rude to us for complaining when we were merely asking when we would be exiting. I now began to experience some nervous symptoms, feeling we were locked in there with no idea when we would be let off. The thoughts were getting worse and I felt like yelling to let us off or at least open the hatch to get some air and know we're not trapped. Thank God I had my Recovery training because I don't know how I would have reacted if I didn't. After about an hour we were finally exiting. I handled myself pretty well and endorsed myself for using the techniques of the Recovery Method. Days and weeks after this event I would constantly think of this incident and would wonder how I would handle a similar event such as that one. Because of these thoughts, I reverted back to my fear of flying.

It was five years before I would get on another plane. There were many more factors that contributed to my mental health setback. I took reassurance in knowing that mental setbacks were inevitable. I knew this because of the training I had received in Recovery. Dr.

Low would talk about setbacks in his writings. He would say, "Expect them. Don't say you have it licked after you've gotten well." He would go on to say, "If you expect them, you won't be disappointed because you also know, what you've done before, you can do again." He was right. It would bother me knowing I was an advocate of the Recovery Method. What would other people think and say? Would they be thinking, "This guy is not only a Group Leader but an Area Leader for all of New York City and he can't even control his own mental health, let alone ours." And, "How good can this Method be, if he is still suffering after all these years?" I felt the veterans who knew the Method well would understand. Some of them had setbacks and would relate with what I was going through. Still, it bothered me knowing the newer members and some who didn't follow the Method very well would feel and think this way. Even here, I used the Recovery Method fairly well. I knew I couldn't control what people thought or said, but I could control myself about how to deal with it.

Sitting at my desk, where I seemed to be most of the time, and thinking of what this organization for which I volunteered a good part of my time was all about, it was a bit difficult right then because I had just recently received a call from a former assistant of mine telling me that her son David had passed away the prior night. Anna is about 78 years old and probably one of the nicest people I have ever known. She now had to tell me that her son died. I don't know how anyone can do that especially after recently losing her husband who was her rock that she leaned on. Now David was gone, probably the closest person in her life since her husband's passing. What was God expecting of her? Hadn't she been through enough? Well, why should I be so surprised? I knew things like this happened and they happened to the very best of people. I'd be going to the funeral the next morning. The Jewish people have about a one hour service and then proceed to the cemetery.

I'll never forget when Artie passed away and I was to attend the service. I had picked up my friend David who was also Jewish and he told me that people mingle for awhile at the time prescribed and then the service begins. We had arrived a few minutes late but felt okay.

## AN OASIS IN THE WILDERNESS

We saw the parking lot was full and street parking was horrendous. And now the traffic was becoming more and more gridlocked. David said, "I'll jump out and see what's going on." As he was doing so, I noticed some cars leaving the parking lot. Within minutes David got back in the car and said the cars were leaving because the service was over. My heart sank and I felt like two cents. "My God, I'm the Area Leader and it's over. How am I going to explain this? And this was Artie, my good friend Artie. And Annie, so sweet, what's she going to think?" Knowing that I would have spoken at the service as a friend and representative of Recovery made me feel even worse. Fortunately, Dave and I made it out to the cemetery and at the gravesite I asked if I could say a few words. They granted my request and I thanked them and also apologized for being late and not being able to speak at the service earlier. Later on that day at home I received a phone call from a lady who attended Recovery meetings. She was appalled that I wasn't at the service. I tried explaining what happened but it was to no avail. She went on lambasting me saying, "This was Artie, and how can you not be there for Artie who has done so much for Recovery and you're the Area Leader?" She went on and on saying things like, "You're like the President, you have to be there." When she made the remark I thought, but did not say, "If I was the President, they all would have waited for me, and then begun the service." Maybe I should have said it. Probably not!

Public speaking was something I would probably never have to worry about doing. Or at least I thought so, and it would be nice to get up in front of a crowd and say things in a way that would really capture their interest. I remember in grammar or junior high school when some of the students were given speeches and taught how to say them. We would then have a contest to see who recited them best. I had studied and practiced my speech until I felt pretty confident I could handle it. When it was my turn, I went up and was feeling very nervous but when I began to speak, I felt I was okay and in control. I even had a thought that I might even win this thing. When I returned back to my seat I asked my teacher how I had done. "Well, you looked good but no one heard you; you were too far away from the microphone." One simple mistake, that's all it took. In a way, it may have been the best thing that could have happened to me. I never forgot it.

Now, when the occasion comes up I practically hug the microphone to death. There was one speech I gave around 2005 that I consider probably the best I ever did. It was at St. Vincent's Hospital in Staten Island. The event director allotted me twenty minutes for my address; everyone else was given about ten to fifteen minutes. I gathered up material that I thought would be appropriate and typed out the most interesting portions to make up a good, well-rounded portrayal of what my organization was all about. I combined reading notes, speaking on the notes I had just read and whatever else I felt would fit in. It worked out pretty well. I was the last one to speak at the morning session. I had to wait and listen to many 12-step organizations such as Alcoholics Anonymous, Overeaters Anonymous and Obsessive Compulsives Anonymous, to name a few. When I got to speak I started with two items I had no idea I would address. I said, "All of you are probably happy to see me, because after I speak we break for lunch." Then I took a chance and said something to the effect of, "After hearing all the organizations before me mention that they are anonymous, I thought I'd just let you know that mine is not anonymous." Then I continued with, "But that's fine, we both have good reasons for being that way." I thought it went over well, and they even gave me a pretty good round of applause when I was finished. Or, could that have been because I was finished? I felt good about how the day transpired but felt a little on the down side because no one from Recovery or friends of mine were there to hear me speak, only a couple of people I knew from the staff that organized the event who told me I did well. It humbled me anyway and I was proud that I did it on my own with no one to hold my hand.

There's one other occasion I must mention where I had to speak. This event took place at the famous Marriott Hotel in Times Square. Mental health organizations from all over the United States were there and we were given tables to display our names and our wares. We went about setting up our table making it look good and felt pleased up to that point. There were some high profile people there. One I remember was Kitty Dukakis, the wife of Michael Dukakis, the fellow who ran for President of the United States. Mrs. Dukakis had written a book and she had many of them there to sell and autograph. I thought of buying one and having her sign it for me but then again I thought, "What am I doing, I'm a Republican, so forget it." As things began, Mrs. Dukakis was the first person to speak. After her were quite a few prominent people with PhDs who also spoke. As the evening wore on we started wondering when I was going to be called up. After Kitty and those high profile people spoke we noticed some people leaving. Finally, the Director of the event came over and told me when I was going to speak. It was just a matter of waiting a little longer, so I thought. We now noticed more and more people leaving and the crowd thinning out. Even the different organizations' tables were being broken down and leaving and we hadn't even spoken yet. When I was told to get ready because I'd be going up soon, I saw that I was positioned next-to-last. I was annoyed that those who were leaving had no consideration for those who hadn't had the opportunity to speak yet. And nobody was doing anything about it. I thought, "By the time I get up there, who's going to be left to listen?" I was angry and thought of some things I would say when I got up there to show my distaste for how insensitive were those who organized this event. I then thought against saying anything derogatory that would only hurt my Recovery organization and make things even worse. I told myself to have a sense of humor and not to take what was happening too seriously. That's what I did and when I went up and started speaking, I noticed my Recovery friends were breaking down our table just as I was pointing it out for the very few people who were still there so they could go over and browse. I thought, "What are they doing and who told them to break down the table?" It was then that I realized how ridiculous this event had turned out and thought how funny it had become. So, with that, I just enjoyed the moment. Months after this event I would have thoughts on it. One of the thoughts was, "Well, at least we weren't last to speak. What's the big deal about being next-to-last?" I felt, and realized, we may have just as well been last. Because last would have been the final indignity. Next-to-last, I believe, is actually worse than being last. If you can't be first or at least near first, you might as well be last because it makes telling this story more interesting, exciting and more amusing. So, here you see, we even got robbed of that!

I'm now in my twenty-fifth year with Recovery. I got to know many people not only in my NYC Area but all over the USA, Canada and a few European countries. There were many successful stories of people with different illnesses. But, of course there are always those stories of sadness. Two good friends of mine, Jack and Selma, passed away just a few years ago. Selma had become ill and when she passed away, Jack must have felt a great loss. They had lived together after both of them had lost their respective spouses. Jack must have felt devastated when Selma was gone. He would have his down moments at times when Selma was alive but at least she was there with him. But now that she was gone, he must have wondered what there was to live for, so he took his own life. Very sad indeed. They were both good company and enjoyable to be with. Many times we would go to a diner after a Recovery meeting and chat, and once in awhile we would go out as a group and have dinner together. They will definitely be missed.

There was another person, Sam, whom most of us didn't know too well but who had begun going out with us to the diner. He had fears of global warming and the burning of the ozone layer. These fears would trigger thoughts of suicide. One time Sam and I got into a conversation a few minutes before the start of my Friday night meeting. It was about different types of suicide that people choose. It wasn't a long conversation by any means, just a few words before the meeting began. Over the weekend I received a call from Marty. He gave me the bad news that Sam had committed suicide. The police found him dead floating on the waters near Coney Island. Ever since that time, I would not want these kinds of conversations to ensue. I was annoyed at myself for speaking to him about suicide and felt I should have known better.

At Recovery meetings you would hear backgrounds of what

members had gone through. Many of these stories were incredible. I found myself wondering how some of these people survived, enduring pain and suffering, feelings of both helplessness and hopelessness, families being broken up, mothers with post-partum depression who feared hurting and harming their children, and those dealing with bipolar disorders talking about the highs and lows and the number of times they attempted suicide. What was so remarkable in many of the lives of these people was the amount of times they were to live, or should I say, survive the agony they had gone through for many years or, for some, most of their lifetime. They are now living normal lives. If I didn't know and saw these people functioning going to supermarkets, banks, restaurants, movie theaters, churches, etc. I would not be able to tell the average person as compared to the person who has dealt with a mental illness.

There have been many advances in the care of people dealing with a mental illness or a nervous affliction. However, there is still a long way to go. There is a stigma attached by society for hundreds of years. It's a very difficult stigma to break and maybe it will never be gone because we are not a perfect society. However, we can reduce it down to a point where it becomes insignificant. I remember someone saying to me, "Did you ever have depression?" When I said, "Yes" he told me, "You should go to a hospital and visit the children's ward." With a remark like that, I could have easily lost my temper. The remark was so provoking and yet I kept my composure and did not argue back with him. Other people were there and I found it inappropriate to engage in an argument. Another reason is my mental health. We learn in Recovery that we cannot afford the luxury of temper and that we shouldn't engage ourselves in going for a symbolic victory which in the end turns out to be an empty victory. I've also learned that if I choose to express myself, I could do it at another time when I'm calm and less emotional. I found the provoking remark to be so typical of how some people think when it comes to mental health issues. To them, it's a simple solution: go to the children's ward and see what these unfortunate kids are going through. This will bring you to your senses and you will realize you really don't have anything to complain about at all. End of problem. You are no longer depressed. It's that simple, right? Wrong! And, it's not the patient who should feel stigmatized; it's society for its take on it. By society separating mental and physical illnesses it perpetrates the separation of the two when it shouldn't. The brain along with the nervous system should not be segregated or therefore, made to look as though it is not a physical condition when in fact it is. If there is a defect in the brain which is considered an organ of the body or a chemical imbalance in a person's anatomy, it should then all be considered as a part of the physical makeup of the human body. It could then be placed in a category that deals with the brain. And that category would be listed under mental health where other categories could be listed as: heart condition, lung condition, kidney condition, etc.

A misconception that many people have (and this includes the patient dealing with a nervous or mental condition) is, are the symptoms real and can they be painful? The answer is yes, the difference being only how these symptoms are being interpreted: heart palpitations, stomach distress, shortness of breath ("air hunger") and so on. You learn in Recovery that symptoms are distressing but are not dangerous. If we go for a physical examination and the doctor tells us there is nothing he or she can find that is bringing on these symptoms, it is then fair to say that the symptoms we are feeling are not dangerous. They are nervous symptoms and not symptoms that are being brought on by a physical ailment of some kind. Some patients go for second, third or more exams not believing the doctors' diagnoses. Some patients refuse to believe there is nothing physically wrong with them. They want the doctor to find something even if it means submitting to an operation. This is where stigma plays a big part. The patient believes this can't be just nerves. "I know what I'm feeling," he would say. Unfortunately, too many people go this route and spend years suffering needlessly for their refusal to believe what the doctor is telling them. When a patient has the conviction to believe what his doctor is telling him is for his own good, then good mental health isn't too far away.

The years seem to be rolling by at what feels like incredible speed.

I'm in my seventies and I suppose this is how most people feel at that age. My participation in Recovery International has dwindled down to being just a regular member. No more group meetings or Leaders' meetings to lead, no more printing ads and meeting lists, taking Recovery phone calls and sending out information to newcomers. I think about all the many psychiatric wards and hospitals I've visited, attending the funerals of our members including members of their families and having to speak and give eulogies at some of them. These are just a few items of my responsibilities in my local Recovery Area as Area Leader. At the national and international level there were no more committees, regional leadership and Board of Directors. Now and then I substitute for some group leaders and do a lot of writing in the area of public relations with many mental health professionals and organizations throughout the world in an effort for these people to learn about and understand what Recovery International and its Recovery Method is all about.

The people I have spoken about in this book, particularly those officials whether volunteers or paid employees, were people I considered to be good and dedicated people. Any criticisms I had, whether positive or negative, are strictly of my own opinion. There were two people who touched me dearly, Kathy Garcia and Mary Gillen. Both passed away soon after most of my Recovery International duties were terminated. I knew Mary had gone for cancer treatments before I got to work with her almost on a daily basis. When she came on as Area Support Director I believe her cancer was in remission. She seemed to be a fighter and wouldn't show any emotion or become sentimental in dealing with her condition. I admired her bravery and hoped that I could handle a condition like that in the unfortunate event I got diagnosed with cancer. When I started to hear people talking about Kathy also being diagnosed with cancer, I tried to deny it. As time went on the talk about Kathy's cancer started getting more and more serious. One time while speaking to her on the phone I said, "Is it true what I've been hearing about you having terminal cancer?" And when she said "yes" I was devastated and thought, "Oh my God, what could I say to her?" I just simply said, "Kathy, I'm so very sorry." She understood and thanked me for my sympathy and we said goodbye. I felt so badly for her and even worse when I thought about some of the controversial issues we'd been disagreeing on lately. I remember her saying on a couple of occasions that she still respected me regardless of whether we disagreed or not. She was a Chicago Cub fan and I, a New York Met fan. She would call them "my Cubbies" and I would say "my Metsies" and we'd make each other's team our second favorite. We had hoped to go to a ballgame together one day while I was in Chicago. Unfortunately it never happened.

Bob MacIntyre (who had been the President of Recovery during most of my time while involved with the International) had our run-ins also. Bob was the one who asked me to chair the ASC and got me on the Board and M&M Committee. He was a decent guy and we got along well with each other. We were both retired blue collar workers, he a machinist and I, an ironworker. One time walking with him to Headquarters I said, "You know, Bob, if someone tried to assassinate you I'd throw myself in front of you and take the bullet." He had a good sense of humor and liked to tell jokes and he was good at it. I remember the night before going to Chicago I got a message that the fellow who was being barred was very upset because he just got manhandled by a group leader and was thrown out of the meeting. When I got the news it was pretty late at night. I wanted to tell Bob but I thought he might have been in Chicago already and, besides, it was late and he was probably sleeping. So, I got in touch with the AL of that Area. We worked out a plan to allow the barred fellow to attend meetings with the exception of one or two groups in the Area. At the time there was some confusion as to whether he was still barred or not. I suggested to the AL that we permit him to go but only for a short period and until Bob and I arrived home from Chicago. The AL agreed. I didn't want to upset this fellow anymore than he was already. I just wanted to play it safe at least until we arrived home and then were able to work on the problem. When I arrived at the hotel in Chicago, Bob MacIntyre was upset with me and on a couple of occasions would let me know it. He would say, "Now let me get this straight, you're the ASC Chair and I'm the President of

Recovery who barred this guy and you're giving permission for him to go to meetings?" He couldn't understand why I was allowing him to go. Even when I told him, "I did it for safety's sake and God only knows what someone may do when they get very angry." I went on to say, "This all happened late at night and I didn't want to wake and frustrate you figuring you probably had so many other things on your mind." He still couldn't understand. I suppose he felt I still couldn't understand. In Recovery we would say this is a "temperamental deadlock," and that "there are no rights or wrongs in the trivialities of everyday life, just differences of opinions." To this day I still think of Bob as a wonderful fellow. He did a lot for Recovery. We may have disagreed a little too much at the end of the day, but I know in our hearts we really wanted to get this organization turned around for all the good that it does.[1]

---

[1] At the time of this writing Bob MacIntyre was still alive. I was informed later of his passing. He will be deeply missed. He was a good guy with a very good heart. God bless him and may he rest in peace.

## CHAPTER 10

# THE THREE, ME AND RECOVERY

There are three individuals who have compelling stories. There are many others I could have chosen who are equally worthy of having their stories told, but somehow these three are outstanding. I got to know two really well; the other is a Jesuit Catholic Priest who has since passed away. His story is just too fascinating to omit. Quite honestly, I feel a whole book could be written about him.

Concetta Natoli:

I received a call one evening and it was my good friend Concetta Natoli, a Recovery member from my group. She was distraught and having an anxiety attack. She was calling from Hungary where she went with her husband to adopt a one year old child. I listened as she went on telling me how nervous she was and how she would not survive this adoption situation. She went on to say how miserable she felt and wanted to come home. "This is my first night here and I can't sleep and don't know how I'm going to make it in the morning when we are to go over and see the baby," she exclaimed. "I'm trying my best to get some sleep but I can't, and I feel as though I'm sabotaging what Dr. Low tells us we should do when this happens, but I just can't." She continued, "We have to stay here for thirty-eight days and I don't know how I'm going to, when I already feel I can't even make it through my first night." Even I was now getting tense. I knew what she had been going through trying to have a baby. "Give her your honest thoughts the best you can, along with what you have learned and experienced since you've been in Recovery," I thought to myself. I went on to tell her to "stop worrying about sabotaging what Dr. Low has taught us because it's only making you get worse. You can still use the Recovery training because of what Low tells us about how unimportant it is at times to have a good night's sleep," and to "remember he also told us that we can still function with little or even no sleep. So, whether you sleep or not, the heck with it. Just go and do what you need to do when you go see the baby. You may be tired and sluggish but that's okay. You may even doze off in the car while being driven there." I went on to say, "You're scaring yourself over lack of sleep and predicting you're going to fail at adopting a child." I also told her to "avoid thinking of the thirty-eight days you'll be spending there. Just take one day at a time and you can even break that into segments of the day. Just concentrate on the moment, not all the moments that lay ahead." As we continued on speaking, I felt she was becoming more and more calm and that made me feel good. When we said goodbye I prayed that she would be okay and I endorsed myself for my efforts.

I had begun thinking back on all that Concetta was going through before going to Hungary to adopt a child. She had attempted three *in vitro* fertilizations and would have gone through a fourth had her doctor not told her it would be dangerous because of her physical condition. Now her thoughts were on adoption. She chose, to my surprise, to go to Europe to adopt. I was surprised because I knew she did not like traveling, especially on a plane and that far. I remember her giving an example at our weekly Recovery meeting and stating, "I would go into symptoms at the thought of even going to my brother's house in New Jersey and staying overnight." And then there she was making plans to go to Hungary and having to stay there for a minimum of thirty-eight days. She went on to say, "Had it not been for the Recovery organization and receiving the training from Dr. Abraham Low's Recovery Method, no way would I be doing this." I did not hear from her the following day or the day after. I didn't know of the outcome, whether she was still in Hungary or not. I just continued to pray until after a week or two I received a letter from her. When I opened the envelope to read it, a picture fell out. When I picked up the picture I started to shed tears. There they were smiling, the three of them, mother, father and their baby boy, Dominick Jr. I was so thrilled to see Concetta pulled through it all. I continued with tears in my eyes as I went on to read her letter:

*Dear Tony,*

*We're here exactly one week and amazingly I'm still here in spite of my symptoms.*

*Thank you from the bottom of my heart, Tony, for caring, being concerned, listening and understanding, and supporting and encouraging me the evening we arrived here. After seeing the baby, I was frazzled, very emotional, symptomatic and overwhelmed. The phone conversation we had that evening helped me tremendously. Who knows if I'd still be here. You helped me to become grounded and that no matter what decision I made you and others who care about me would understand. I took your advice and I'm literally part acting every minute, hour, day, etc. And my main focus is on calming down my inner environment and continuing to function as I've done in the past in spite of my symptoms. I'm also placing my mental health and inner peace as my #1 priority because without it I cannot function. Thank you for being there and knowing that you're there for me should I need extra support, is a very secure thought.*

*Little Dominick is a very special and beautiful little boy who happens to have an excellent disposition. He seems to be a really good baby. He's extremely happy, well adjusted and smiles and laughs a lot. He crawls all over the place and is amazed with everything and everyone around him. He seems to have taken to us very well and we're beginning to really care for him and love him even though we don't feel like Mommy and Daddy yet. I guess that takes time and it will happen sometime soon when we're ready. Perhaps because we're still bringing him back to his foster parents every evening could have a lot to do with it. On Thursday Dec. 20 he will be ours for good. We will go to Budapest for the remainder of our journey. I miss you and everyone in Recovery dearly. Please send my love and regards to everyone. Enjoy the photos and please show everyone if you like.*

*All our Love*

*Concetta, Dominick and Little Dominick, Our Son*

Bob Graziano:

I think the longest running friendship I've had in Recovery Inc. has been with Bob Graziano. He was at my first meeting in October 1990 but I didn't get to know him until after my Hawaii trip, which was probably my second or third meeting. He had asked me if I could drop him off at the bus stop. Little did I know this would be the start of a friendship that is still going on to this day, twenty-six years later. Shortly after dropping him off at the bus stop, I began to drive him home. Home for him was a halfway house in East New

York, Brooklyn, not such a great place to live in. The neighborhood was essentially a minority neighborhood with a high crime rate. Bob had been diagnosed with paranoid schizophrenia. The people that lived at the halfway house (also known as an adult home) were there because of a number of reasons: mental illness, drug and alcohol addiction, poverty, etc. It is not the kind of place you would ever want to be. During the years that I have known him, he has moved around to other similar facilities and also taken part in supportive living apartment programs. The apartment programs are where one shares an apartment with a couple of other people with similar problems. Bob's been in and out of psychiatric hospitals a number of times, and for several months lived at a place in Staten Island, NY called South Beach Psychiatric Center. South Beach reminded me somewhat of a military compound. While there, he was restricted from leaving the area. He even had to ask for permission to step outside to get a little fresh air. I visited him at all these places and, usually, more than once. Some I dreaded going to. The worst place was Kings County Psychiatric Center. Everything about it was ugly. A few years back there was a story in the news about a female patient slipping off a chair while waiting to receive her medication. She had been left lying on the floor for hours even while an attendant was able to see her but did nothing. Eventually, she was looked at, and it was determined she was dead. I don't understand why they waited so long to look after her. All this was captured by security cameras. The only thing I could think of is probably the people who work at these places must see an awful lot that most of us would not be able to take. Maybe the job becomes too routine there, and learning to not bother at times when someone is lying on the floor happens continuously. Nevertheless, it should be no excuse.

Another place I visited and thought was quite shabby was Coney Island Hospital. This place was an adventure and quite amusing after a few frustrating moments. I had gone up the elevator and when the door opened there was a gate that had to be opened by an attendant before you could step out. When the attendant opened it a few people stepped out but when I tried to step out, the attendant stopped me.

When he asked me what I wanted, I said, "I'd like to visit a friend of mine." He said, "Visiting hours are over, please step back in." The elevator went back down but I didn't get off. I pressed the button and went back up. As the door opened the attendant saw it was me again and said, "I told you visiting hours are over." I said, "I know you did, but my friend must have made a mistake and gave me the wrong time for visiting hours." He said, "Sorry, I can't let you in." He made sure I was going back down again. Feeling frustrated and a bit angry, I pressed the button and went back up a third time. This time when the door opened, the gate was also opened so I stepped out and started to walk down the hall trying to avoid the attendant, but he caught up to me. At least this time I was standing in the hallway and not in the elevator. I told him, "The person I want to see is a patient and a member of my organization and I'm here because it's my responsibility as Area Leader of New York City for Recovery Inc. to look after our patients' mental health." With that he brought me to a glass-enclosed staff station and told me to say who I wanted to see and who I was. I thanked him and stepped inside. I was asked, "Does Bob Graziano know you?" I said, "Yes, he does." I waited while the attendant told some people to check on Bob. He then asked again, "Does he know you?" And again after that. Every time he asked me, I told him, "Yes, he knows me." Getting tired of this fellow asking me repeatedly, I suddenly heard a voice in a loud tone say, "Hey Tony, that's you? Tony, that's you?" I looked and there was Bob walking over to the door. With that, I looked at the attendant and said with a big smile on my face, "Does he know me?"

When I would visit Bob at these places he would usually say to me, "I don't like it here Tony, I want to get out." My usual advice to him would be to avoid complaining. "If someone is bothering you and you begin to argue that's not good and if someone comes over to you and for no good reason gets mad or wants to start a fight, walk away." I continued, "If you get into it with another patient regardless of who is right or wrong, avoid it by all means. The reason I'm saying this is because the staff and attendants a lot of times just observe you guys fighting. And in most cases, they don't know who started it; all they see is you and the other person fighting." I would finish up with, "So, what I'm saying is, even though you are right and the other person started the fight, they may write you up anyway. And when it's time to evaluate your condition, it could be held against you. So, keep that in mind if you want to get out."

There was very little contact between Bob and his family. He wasn't permitted to go home to the house in which he grew up. From what I understood, there was an incident where he pushed his mother and she fell down. That's all I ever knew and this was before I got to know him. His father, a retired police officer, was deceased. He had died from a brain aneurism. Bob would tell me about his father who it seems took care of him most of the time. Although his father was a bit of a hard-nosed kind of guy, I felt Bob loved him and missed him. He had a younger sister but had no idea where she lived, although he knew she had gotten married. There was one person he was able to see and that was his grandmother. He loved his grandmother and would travel out to see her now and then. She was in a nursing home in Long Island, NY. It always amazed me at some of the things mentally ill patients were able to do. Bob had no problem traveling, taking buses, the subway and the Long Island Railroad when he'd go to see his grandmother, or for that matter, anywhere else. Simple everyday things, however, were difficult. He's a very intelligent person, even earning himself a college degree in business, something I never did. I considered myself lucky just to graduate high school. Bob would actually help a lot with my English and in other areas quite a bit and when he did, it was not at all to show me up. He's a very considerate person to others. He loves sports and is very knowledgeable. I always enjoy talking sports with him especially when it's about our favorite team, the New York Mets.

Bob has grown to be more reserved now. He calls maybe a few times each week, a far cry from when he would call about three or four times a day. There were occasions when I would get irritated with him and we would argue, not much today but during the early days when we would see more of each other. There was one time when he called me and asked if I could come to his place and lend him some money. I told him I was very tired and not looking to do anything or go anywhere. He kept insisting that I come over because he needed to buy medication. I was so annoyed with him that I was raising my voice and saying some things to him that must have hurt his feelings. I finally told him, "Okay, okay, I'll be there" and hung up the phone. When I arrived he was walking out of his residence and met me at the entrance door. He was upset and complaining to me that I shouldn't have spoken to him on the phone in such a mean way. I said, "I can't believe you! I go out of my way being dead tired to come here and give you the money, and you're getting angry with me because of what I said on the phone and how I said it?" He looked at me and started to defend himself. There we were, both of us arguing out on the sidewalk by my car at night when I gave him the money then said, "You got the money, now leave me the hell alone and don't bother with me anymore." I jumped in the car and as I drove down a couple of blocks feeling upset at what just happened, I started to think of something funny. I thought, "Wow, what if the cops came out here to break us up?" I thought again and started to laugh silently because of the police maybe thinking, "What in the world is going on here, two white guys arguing out in the street in a minority neighborhood? What are the chances of that happening?"

There were a few times when I thought the friendship between Bob and me would end but it never did. In the 1990s for a good many years I would go out on Sunday mornings each week and pick up Bob and we'd go out to a diner and have breakfast. Most of the time he would pay his own way. Over the last ten or so years we no longer got together every week; now it would be about once every one or two months. Only now I would treat him to breakfast. He would always try to give me some money but I would tell him not to worry about it. If he insisted on giving me a dollar or two, I would sometimes take it. I know he had his pride and would want to pay on his own. When it comes to money he is limited to what he is allowed to have. He receives a medical pension for the eleven years he had worked for the US Post Office. However, his money does not go to him, but rather to the NYS Office of Mental Health to pay for his lodging and upkeep.

Although he receives an allowance, it's a modest amount which limits him on what he can spend.

There were times when he would come into receiving a little cash for various reasons. I remember holding on to some of his money and would give whatever he would need whenever he would be a little short on cash. If what little he had was put into savings or checking accounts it probably would be garnished by the State agency. He actually had some money in a bank account one time that had to be closed. The money that was in the account went to the State of New York that was paying for his upkeep. However, he was allowed to take $1,500.00 to put toward a burial account for himself. One time I opened a safe deposit box at a bank near where he lived in case he needed a few bucks. Having any money stored in his bedroom for safekeeping was not a good idea. You'd probably kiss it goodbye in a couple of days for obvious reasons.

There was one day that I'll never forget for all the twists and turns it took that even a Hollywood comedy screenwriter would not even think of putting in a script. Bob called me and told me he received a letter from the bank with whom he had previously closed all his accounts. The bank was located in Mill Basin, the neighborhood he grew up in and also where I just happen to live. It was about a safe deposit box that was in his name. The letter went on to say that the rental fees hadn't been paid in quite a long time. And, the fee added up to $85.00 and would rise even higher because of the late fees. We thought of ignoring it because there was probably nothing in it. However, we really didn't know that for sure. If we went there to close it, the $85.00 fee would have to be paid before we opened the box. We thought, "Could it contain money or something valuable, or would it be just an empty box?" The only way for us to find out was to pay the fee. The problem with that was, Bob didn't have the $85.00. Here I was again getting myself involved with someone else's problem and thinking, "Should I lend him the money knowing I may not get it back or just let him deal with the problem and stay out of it?" I thought again, "How in the heck do I get myself into these things?" Well, I decided to lend him the money and take the chance.

When I asked him about the key to the box, he said, "I don't have a key, I don't remember having a key." "Okay, what else is going to happen?" I thought to myself. I called the bank and told them Bob didn't have the key and asked what could be done. I was told we would have to pay a locksmith to open it and there was a fee for that also. We made an appointment with the bank to have this taken care of. On the day of the appointment, I picked up Bob and we went to the bank. While waiting for the locksmith, I sat down with the bank manager to ask him if he could give Bob a break on the fee considering his disabilities. I had no luck with that either, but I tried and endorsed myself for the effort. While the locksmith drilled out the key slot of the box I kept hoping there was enough money in it to pay for all this. Waiting there made me think of the big deal that was made on TV when they were to open Al Capone's safe, only to find it empty. The locksmith had finished and we were permitted to go in and check out the box. When we did so, we both let out a sigh of relief. There was cash there, and it looked like there was enough to pay the expenses of it all. Thank God! We counted it and then I took what was owed to me and we left.

As we drove away we talked about what we would do with the money. It was decided we'd put it all in the safe deposit box I had opened in Borough Park, Brooklyn, where he was living at the time. When we got to the bank, I told him, "Okay, be careful, and put the money in the box, I'm going home." I left, felt glad that was over with, and went home. A little later I receive a call from Bob. He sounded somewhat flustered. "Tony, when I put my hands in my pocket I'm pulling out a lot of money," When I asked him, "What money are you talking about?" He said, "I don't know." I said, "Didn't you put the money in the safe deposit box when I dropped you off?" He said, "Yes." "So, where did this money come from?" I asked. He said, "I don't know." "How much do you have?" "I don't know," he said again. By this time I was getting a bit worked up and annoyed with myself thinking back to when I dropped him off at the bank and didn't go in with him. Why didn't I go in with him? I should have gone in with him. Then I told him, "Listen, I have to lead my Recovery meeting tonight. Leave early, be careful and bring the money with you and I'll hold onto it for you." He said, "Okay."

Our meeting was in the Saint Bernard's Parish rectory. Bob did come early and I met him in the hallway between the rectory office (which no one was in at the time) and the meeting room. As he approached me, I said, "Do you have the money?" "Yes," he said. He then went reaching into his pockets and pulling out cash. The cash was not neatly together; it was more like in chunks with different denominations. As I was taking it from him and trying to straighten out and count the bills I realized, "What if the priest walks by and sees us? This is not going to look good, it looks like one of those scenes from the movies of a drug deal going down," I told Bob to go into the meeting room and wait there while I went into the bathroom to count the money. It was difficult trying to count it the way it was all crumbled up. I started to feel a little anxiety coming on but I gave myself a secure thought that the bathroom door was locked and I could relax knowing I didn't have to fear someone seeing me. I put the toilet seat cover down so the money wouldn't fall in and used the top of the toilet tank to separate the different denominations. I counted it and it came to several hundred dollars. I put it neatly into my pockets, led the meeting, drove Bob home and told him that I would hold it for him until whenever he might need some. He was fine with me suggesting that.

I still see Bob at times, usually every month or two on Sunday mornings. We go out for breakfast and just relax for awhile and talk sports. He's living at a place in Bath Beach, Brooklyn which is not too bad of a neighborhood and he has a roommate with whom he gets along with pretty well, unlike at most of the other places he's been. He also hears from his sister every now and then, who's living in North Carolina with her husband and three young children. He sees her maybe once or twice a year. I was fortunate to meet her and her lovely family one day when we went out for pizza. I'm very glad for Bob that life has become much more tolerable, which in turn seems to have made him much more content. He deserves it especially after all he has endured.

Father Bernie Shannon:

One day a friend of mine handed me an article written by Bill Reel from a local newspaper in New York. The article was about Father Bernie Shannon, a Catholic priest. After reading it I thought, "Wow, what a story." In the article it mentioned our organization, Recovery Inc., and how it helped Fr. Shannon regain his mental health. I remember thinking about how someone like this could be an inspiration to so many people. The people I knew in Recovery Inc. including myself were average people in the local community who were learning and being trained in how to use the Recovery Method to get well just like Fr. Shannon had done. One big difference, though, with Fr. Shannon was that he became a priest and was very open about mental illness, not only to those who attended mass and other services at Saint Ignatius Retreat House in Manhasset, NY where he was living, but on the lecture circuit as well. He would spread the word about not being afraid of speaking about one's mental health and the stigma society had placed upon it. Father Shannon took advantage of his opportunities speaking with large groups of people, whereas most of us in Recovery did not have such opportunities. He was able to speak of his bouts dealing with mental illness even during the 8 AM morning mass services he administered in the basement chapel. Even after the service, he would follow up by welcoming and inviting the congregation to join him for breakfast upstairs in the dining room.

I, along with my Recovery friends from Brooklyn, had gotten together on a few occasions and gone out to the Retreat House and attended Fr. Shannon's 8 AM service and then joined with him during the breakfast that followed. Prior to one of these occasions I had called him asking for permission to bring my camcorder and video tape the 8 AM service. He graciously granted me permission. When we arrived and went to the chapel, I took out the camcorder and was prepared to take the video. Fr. Shannon asked me to give him a minute or two to speak to the congregation and tell them I would be videotaping the service and if there was anyone who might be uncomfortable because of it, perhaps they could move to the rear. When I saw a woman stand up and start walking toward the rear, I stood up myself and told Fr. Shannon, "That's okay, I won't take the video." I think he appreciated my concern for others, although one of my friends told me after the service, "You should have taken it and not worry about the lady." However, I asked the Father if I could shoot a video upstairs with him being interviewed by Lynn from our group. He agreed and it worked out really well. Lynn asked, "Father Shannon, could you please tell us what brought you into Recovery Inc.?" As it turned out, that was the only question Lynn needed to ask. Why? Because when he looked into the camera and began to speak, he went on for several minutes and said just about everything that needed to be said.

He spoke about his mental condition and his breakdown while attending the seminary in his younger years. When he would be taken to a hospital he would become violent and would have to be restrained in a straight jacket to keep him under control. And during his stays at the hospital he would be put into restraints at times because he wanted so much to get at the guards and beat them. When he would be brought back to the seminary he was told at times he would not be able to become a priest because of his mental illness. Then one day he was told by three lady friends about a self-help organization called Recovery Inc. and that they felt he could really get help there. He said, "I took their advice and went to a couple of meetings and then stopped. When I met up one day with the ladies again they asked if I had gone there, I told them, 'I did, but stopped after attending two or three meetings.'" They then told him, "Oh no, that's not enough" and then said, "You should go for at least six to eight meetings to get a good idea of the help you can get." With that, he said he started going again and began to see other members there who were getting well. He thought, "If they can get well maybe I could also." "So, I continued to go and get the training and then started feeling I was improving every time I went." He said he marveled at how Dr. Low could have come up with a method that was unique and so practical and simple to understand. He said, "I knew, then, why Dr. Low would tell his patients that the Method was simple but not easy. Just merely knowing it was not enough, you had to practice it." Be an apprentice and go through the training," as Low would say. With the training Fr. Shannon said he improved to the point where he was able to function as well as the average person and deal with whatever life threw at him. He was now able to complete his studies to become a priest. With a special dispensation awarded him by the Pope he said, "I was ordained a priest in 1980 by Cardinal Cook after thirty-three years at the seminary."

He ended by saying, "I have a picture of Dr. Low hanging up on my bedroom wall," and followed up by saying, "It took a Jewish doctor to make me a Catholic priest."

# THE MISCONCEPTIONS OF MENTAL ILLNESS AND THE STIGMA THAT FOLLOWS (EDUCATING THE PATIENT AS WELL AS SOCIETY)

*Essay by Tony Ferrigno[2]*

Mental illness is probably the most misunderstood and abused medical condition. At one time it was an illness that no one would dare talk about. The stigma was so strong it was looked upon as a crime. Patients would be "put away," not necessarily to be treated, but to shield them from the public. It was an illness to be ashamed of, cursed with, and brought upon by the patients themselves. It was looked upon as anti-social behavior, poor upbringing or simply a damning disease. A patient of the late neuropsychiatrist, Abraham Low, founder of Recovery International (RI) and the Recovery Method (a group-based, peer-led cognitive behavioral training program), asked, "Why should there be a distinction between people who are sick above the neck and those sick below the neck?" ("My Dear Ones"

---

[2] This essay was submitted in a contest conducted by the International Mental Health Research Organization in response to the question "What one update to the national mental health policy would you like to see instituted in the next five years, and why?"

by Neil and Margaret Rau, p. 76). They all knew the answer; it was society who didn't.

In 1937, two years after the inception of Alcoholics Anonymous, RI was established as the first mental health self-help organization. It did not become part of the Anonymous programs but has its own very original approach to managing mental illness, while also combating stigma. Proud of being part of RI, I salute "Bring Change2 Mind" for its anti-stigma crusade for mental illness.

I have often wondered why mental illness tends to be segregated from physiological illnesses such as diabetes, cancer, or a heart condition. If the brain is a physical organ of the body and a chemical reaction (blood and fluids) also of the physical anatomy, then wouldn't it all be considered physiological? "Physical" connotes being seen and felt and is relatively simple to explain; whereas, "mental" is thought of as theoretical, which cannot be seen or felt and is therefore more complicated and difficult to explain. Mental illness is thus subject to scrutiny and abuse which causes the patient to delay pursuit of help. On the contrary, Dr. Low saw mental illness as a physiological condition and developed a mental health management training method in addition to offering medical treatment. As a patient and veteran group Leader for Recovery International I have encountered many patients including myself who, because of lack of education or ignorance, made getting well more difficult than needed to be. Non-compliance with medications and treatment is a frequent issue for patients suffering from mental illness. Resisting the professional's advice initiates the long and arduous road for the patient. Patients often make decisions solely on what they feel they need, not what an educated professional tells them. They refuse to take medication simply because "it's a drug and drugs do harm" or, if on medication, they don't take seriously what is prescribed. Given therapy, they frequently sabotage simply because they disagree or believe they know better. Then, there is the other extreme: patients who make a ritual of changing doctors but continue to believe "they don't understand me," or "who knows my body better than I?"

This self-sabotage may lead to many years of needless pain and suffering. And that is why I chose to write about commencement of mental health education programs in schools and follow-up with refresher courses in later years. By instituting such an initiative, it would not only help the patient or prospective patient, but would also assist the general public in having a better understanding of the illness and reduce the stigma to a minimum.

In just about all cases, people seeking medical care, with the exception of those dealing with a mental illness, are referred to as "patients," not "clients." I believe it is time for a cultural change where all receiving medical care should be referred to as "patients." As much as we would like to eliminate stigma from mental illness, we ourselves may be holding on to it more than we are aware.

I believe the choice should be left to the individual to decide whether he wants to be referred to as a "patient" or "client," although an explanation can be given by the professional as to why in the mental health field "client" is predominantly used rather than "patient." However, to combat the stigma that is attached to mental health issues, the patient should be given the choice in deciding. It can be explained that there shouldn't be any shame or embarrassment in dealing with mental illness as there isn't any in the field of physical illnesses. Being a realist and knowing the patient may be uncomfortable especially in the early stages it's okay to go with whatever the individual chooses.

Another point to mention is our choice of language. We sometimes don't realize how we, like others, hold onto stigma. If we say something such as, "Joe is schizophrenic" it connotes only one characteristic. Joe will most likely have other attributes such as: "Joe is a likeable guy" or "he's good at what he does," etc. However, if "Joe is dealing with schizophrenia," is substituted he is not deprived of any additional characteristics and the stigma is hopefully dropped.

Much has been accomplished to combat the stigma of mental illness, but we still have a long way to go.

# PART 2

Chapter 12: What is The Recovery Method and What is
Cognitive Behavioral Therapy?............................97
Chapter 13: Comparison of Cognitive Behavioral Therapy
(CBT) and The Recovery Method (RM)................ 110
Chapter 14: Who Thought of CBT and How Did it Originate?.... 118
Chapter 15: Discussions on Mental Health Topics
From the CBT Networking For
Professional Therapists Website................................128
Chapter 16: Recovery Method Mental Health Tools to Live By....156

# CHAPTER 12

# WHAT IS THE RECOVERY METHOD AND WHAT IS COGNITIVE BEHAVIORAL THERAPY?

*Note: I will comment first on my personal opinion and the opinion of many others I know who believe Dr. Abraham Low was the first person to usher in what is known today as: Cognitive Behavioral Therapy. After my comments I will go into explaining, "What is the Recovery Method?" and then, "What is Cognitive Behavioral Therapy?"*

    I have been told by professionals from time to time that they haven't heard about neuropsychiatrist Abraham Low and the Recovery Method which he developed in the 1930s and, without question, is still as good today as it was back then. I believe that Low was the first person to devise a method that ushered in what today is referred to as Cognitive Behavioral Therapy. Unfortunately, he was not well recognized for his outstanding work which has given thousands upon thousands of those suffering with a mental illness a chance to regain their lives back and be able to function in daily life.

Credit was given to well known people such as, Albert Ellis, Aaron Beck and other prominent names that followed after Dr. Abraham Low. The method that was popular and used by many professionals in the early Twentieth Century was the Freudian psychoanalysis method. Dr. Low was taught this method and practiced it during his early days as a neuropsychiatrist.

Using this method had helped his patients. Unfortunately, he was only to learn that many of them had once again, fallen victim to relapses that put them back in hospitals and returned them back to his practice. Low began to see this repeatedly and referred to it as a revolving door syndrome which consumed a lot of time and a lot of money, which most patients weren't able to afford. Witnessing what was deemed as the inevitable, Low discarded the Freudian method and began to practice his well-thought-out Recovery Method. His Method was so successful, he attempted to have it introduced and practiced at state hospitals in Illinois to the point of almost losing his medical license. He received little to no support from many of his own peers. I believe it came down to the old saying, "Why bite the hand that is feeding you?"

As I stated above, it's unfortunate that many professionals haven't heard of Dr. Abraham Low and the Recovery Method. I've had many clinicians tell me that very little to nothing was brought out or taught in colleges and universities about Low. To me and many of my fellow peers we see this as a travesty or blight (if I may) on the psychiatric profession. I, however, sincerely hope that one day that blight is removed from this honorable profession and Dr. Low be finally recognized and respected for all that he accomplished in helping mankind.

In Recovery International, we use the Recovery Method (RM). We talk about CBT as being similar to RM and as I commented previously, many of us believe that is what brought about CBT. However, we as patients, clients or members of Recovery International, also realize that we are not professionals trained to administer therapy but we are trained at our local community self-help group meetings to learn and understand the Recovery Method and above all practice it. As we become veteran members, we are able to pass it onto newer members.

**What is the Recovery Method?**

The Recovery Method is a system of cognitive techniques for controlling behavior and changing attitudes toward symptoms and fears. People who practice the Method learn to change their thoughts and behaviors; changes in attitudes and beliefs will follow. The Recovery Method is explained in Dr. Low's book, "Mental Health Through Will-Training" (MHTWT) and other writings. In MHTWT, Dr. Low starts with what he refers to as: "A Concise Outline of Recovery's Self-Help Techniques." I've included four of what I consider his main components of the Recovery Method: The Symptomatic Idiom, The Temperamental Lingo, The Recovery Language and The Spotting Technique.[3]

Four of the main components of "A Concise Outline of Recovery's Self-Help Techniques"

1. The Symptomatic Idiom:

If the patients are to help and teach one another they must be instructed to use a language which is not confusing. This is particularly important because language, if used glibly, tends to be alarmist and defeatist. By dint of its defeatist insinuations, language frequently engenders tenseness, which reinforces and perpetuates symptoms. To avoid the fatalistic implications of the language used by the patient the physician must supply a terminology of his own in matters of health. There are many languages. Features and gestures speak. So

---

[3] The Concise Outline of Recovery's Self-Help Techniques was taken from the book, "Mental Health Through Will-Training," authored by Dr. Abraham Low, founder of the Recovery Method and Recovery Inc., later renamed Recovery International

do symptoms. Their language is a one word idiom: DANGER. This is called the "symptomatic idiom." Accepting the suggestions of the symptomatic idiom the patient considers the violent palpitations as presaging sudden death. The pressure in the head is viewed as due to a brain tumor. The tenseness is experienced as so "terrific" that the patient fears he is going to "burst." His fatigue does not let up "one single minute," and "how long can the body stand it?" In these instances, the implications of the symptomatic idiom are those of an impending *physical collapse*. If phobias, compulsions and obsessions dominate the symptomatic scene the resulting fear is that of the *mental collapse*. After months and years of sustained suffering the twin fears of physical and mental collapse may recede, giving way to apprehensions about the impossibility of a final cure. This is the fear of the *permanent handicap*. The three basic fears of the physical collapse, mental collapse and permanent handicap are variations of the danger theme suggested by the symptomatic idiom.

2. The Temperamental Lingo:

Another source of defeatism is temper. The patients are taught that temper has two divisions. The one comes into play when I persuade myself that a person has done me wrong. As a result I become angry. This is called the angry or aggressive temper, which appears in various shades and nuances: resentment, impatience, indignation, disgust, hatred, etc. The other variety of temper is brought into action whenever I feel that I am wrong. This gives rise to moral, ethical and esthetic fears or to the fear of being a failure in pragmatic pursuits. I am afraid I have sinned, failed, blundered, in short, that I defaulted on a moral, ethical or esthetic standard or on the standard of average efficiency. This is called the *fearful or retreating temper* which may express itself in many different qualities and intensities: discouragement, preoccupation, embarrassment, despair, etc. The fearful temper is likely to lead either to a feeling of personal inferiority or to the sentiment of group stigmatization. Whether it's of the angry or fearful description, temper reinforces and intensifies the symptom which, in its turn, increases the temperamental reaction. In this manner, a vicious cycle is established between temper and symptom. The temperamental reaction is kept alive mainly by the unsympathetic and unthinking attitude of the relatives. By means of coarse statements or subtle innuendo they provoke loud explosions or silent agonies on the part of the patient. They tell him to use his will power, implying that he makes no effort to get well. With this, they indict him as a weakling, worse yet, as purposely shamming disease. They urge him to "snap out of it," indicating that the symptoms are so easy to deal with that a mere snap would shake them out of existence. Other insinuations frequently leveled against the psychoneurotic or former mental patient are equally disconcerting. Complaining of fatigue he is told not to be lazy; mentioning his "awful palpitations," he is admonished to be a man. The net result of this concerted environmental assault is that the patient is continually angry at his detractors and, gradually accepting their insinuations, he becomes ashamed and fearful of himself.

In telling the patient that wrong was done to him or that he is wrong, his temper speaks to him. The language which is used is called the *temperamental lingo*. Its vocabulary is limited to the terms "right" and "wrong." Unless the patient learns to ignore the threats, warnings and incitements of the temperamental lingo he will be the victim of angry outbursts and fearful anticipation. His tenseness will be maintained and intensified; new symptoms will be precipitated and old ones fortified. Temper is most dangerous when it plays on the symptom itself. By labeling sensations as "intolerable," feelings as "terrible," impulses as "uncontrollable" the lingo discourages the patient from facing, tolerating and controlling the reaction. The very sound of the labels ("intolerable," etc.) is apt to arouse fear and defeatism. All a patient has to do is call a crying reaction by the name of "crying spell," and no effort will be made to check the burst of tears. The word "spell" suggests uncontrollability. Make the patient substitute "crying habit" for "crying spell," and the impossibility of stemming the flood at least will not be taken for granted. Similarly, if the patient raves about the "splitting" headache, the dizziness that "drives me mad," the pressure that "I can't stand any longer," the fatalism of diction is bound to breed a despondency of mood. In order to prevent the temperamental response the patient must be trained to ignore the whispering of his temperamental lingo.

3. The "Recovery Language":

The combined effects of symptomatic idiom and temperamental lingo are checkmated if the patient is made to use the physician's language only. The members of the association call it proudly the "Recovery Language." The most important parts of its vocabulary are the words: "sabotage" and "authority." The authority of the physician is sabotaged if the patient presumes to make a diagnostic, therapeutic or prognostic statement. The verbiage of the temperamental lingo ("unbearable," "intolerable," "uncontrollable") constitutes sabotage because of the assumption that the condition is of a serious nature which is a diagnosis; or, that it is difficult to repair, which is a prognosis. It is a classic example of sabotage if the claim is advanced that, "my headache is there the very minute I wake up. I didn't have time to think about it. It came even before I had a chance to become emotional. How can that be nervous?" A statement of this kind throws a serious doubt on the validity of the physician's diagnosis and sabotages his authority. Likewise, it is a case of self-diagnosing and consequently sabotage to view palpitations as a sign of heart ailment, of head pressure as meaning brain tumor, of sustained fatigue as leading to a physical exhaustion. Once the physician has made the diagnosis of a psychoneurotic or post-psychotic condition the patient is no longer permitted to indulge in the pastime of self-diagnosing. If he does he is practicing sabotage. Patients are expected to lose their major symptoms after two months of Recovery membership and class attendance. If after the two month period the handicap persists in its original intensity the indication is that sabotage is still in action. The patient still listens to the suggestion of the symptomatic idiom fearing impending collapse and permanent handicap. Or, he gives ear to the verbal vagaries of the temperamental lingo, feeling helpless in the face of suffering. Clinging to his own mode of thinking he sabotages the physician's effort.

Contrary to expectations, it is comforting to the patient to be called a saboteur. Considering himself as such he knows that he has "not yet" learned to avoid resisting the physician. The "not yet" is reassuring. It suggests that in time he will learn. The patients encourage one another to wait until they get well. They warn one another against impatience. The most effective slogan handed down from veteran to novice is, "Wait till you will learn to give up sabotaging."

4. The Spotting Technique:

If the patient is to check his sabotaging propensities he must be trained to "spot" the inconsistencies and fallacies of his own language whether it is merely conceived in silent thought or given formulation in vocal speech. To this end, a system of "spotting techniques" was evolved by means of which the members learn to reject the suggestion of the symptomatic idiom and the temperamental lingo whenever a symptom or a temperamental reaction occurs.

**What is Cognitive Behavioral Therapy?**

*Note: I've checked on the web to see what some well known mental health organizations had to say on their description of "What is CBT?" I've chosen two that I thought would make a good comparison and included it below.*

National Association of Cognitive Behavioral Therapists:[4]

Cognitive-Behavioral Therapy is a form of psychotherapy that emphasizes the important role of thinking in how we feel and what we do. Cognitive-behavioral therapy does not exist as a distinct therapeutic technique. The term "cognitive-behavioral therapy" (CBT) is a very general term for a classification of therapies with similarities. There are several approaches to cognitive-behavioral therapy, including Rational Emotive Behavior Therapy, Rational Behavior Therapy, Rational Living Therapy, Cognitive Therapy, and Dialectic Behavior Therapy. However, most cognitive-behavioral therapies have the following characteristics:

1. CBT is based on the Cognitive Model of Emotional Response.
2. CBT is briefer and time-limited.
3. A sound therapeutic relationship is necessary for effective therapy, but not the focus.
4. CBT is a collaborative effort between the therapist and the client.
5. CBT is based on aspects of stoic philosophy.
6. CBT uses the Socratic Method.
7. CBT is structured and directive.
8. CBT is based on an educational model.
9. CBT theory and techniques rely on the Inductive Method.
10. Homework is a central feature of CBT.

1. **CBT is based on the Cognitive Model of Emotional Response.**

Cognitive-behavioral therapy is based on the idea that our *thoughts* cause our feelings and behaviors, not external things, like people, situations, and events. The benefit of this fact is that we can change the way we think to feel / act better even if the situation does not change.

---

[4] The National Association of Cognitive-Behavioral Therapists has given its consent to include its description of "What is CBT?"

2. **CBT is briefer and time-limited.**

Cognitive-behavioral therapy is considered among the most rapid in terms of results obtained. The average number of sessions clients receive (across all types of problems and approaches to CBT) is only 16. Other forms of therapy, like psychoanalysis, can take years. What enables CBT to be briefer are its highly instructive nature and the fact that it makes use of homework assignments. CBT is time-limited in that we help clients understand at the very beginning of the therapy process that there will be a point when the formal therapy will end. The ending of the formal therapy is a decision made by the therapist and client. Therefore, CBT is not an open-ended, never-ending process.

3. **A sound therapeutic relationship is necessary for effective therapy, but not the focus.**

Some forms of therapy assume that the main reason people get better in therapy is because of the positive relationship between the therapist and client. Cognitive-behavioral therapists believe it is important to have a good, trusting relationship, but that is not enough. CBT therapists believe that the clients change because they learn how to think differently and they act on that learning. Therefore, CBT therapists focus on teaching rational self-counseling skills.

4. **CBT is a collaborative effort between the therapist and the client.**

Cognitive-behavioral therapists seek to learn what their clients want out of life (their goals) and then help their clients achieve those goals. The therapist's role is to listen, teach, and encourage, while the client's role is to express concern, learn, and implement that learning.

5. **CBT is based on aspects of stoic philosophy.**

Not all approaches to CBT emphasize stoicism. Rational Emotive Behavior Therapy, Rational Behavior Therapy, and Rational Living Therapy emphasize aspects of stoicism. Beck's Cognitive Therapy is not based on stoicism. Cognitive-behavioral therapy does not tell people how they should feel. However, most people seeking therapy do not want to feel the way they have been feeling. The approaches that emphasize stoicism teach the benefits of feeling, at worst, *calm* when confronted with undesirable situations. They also emphasize the fact that we have our undesirable situations whether we are upset about them or not. If we are upset about our problems, we have two problems — the problem, and our upset about it. Most people want to have the fewest number of problems possible. So when we learn how to more calmly accept a personal problem, not only do we feel better, but we usually put ourselves in a better position to make use of our intelligence, knowledge, energy, and resources to resolve the problem.

6. **CBT uses the Socratic Method.**

Cognitive-behavioral therapists want to gain a very good understanding of their clients' concerns. That's why they often ask *questions*. They also encourage their clients to ask questions of themselves, like, "How do I really know that those people are laughing at me? Could they be laughing about something else?"

7. **CBT is structured and directive.**

Cognitive-behavioral therapists have a specific agenda for each session. Specific techniques / concepts are taught during each session. CBT focuses on the client's goals. We do not tell our clients what their goals "should" be, or what they "should" tolerate. We are directive in the sense that we show our clients how to think and behave in ways to obtain what they want. Therefore, CBT therapists do not tell their clients *what* to do — rather, they teach their clients *how* to do.

8. **CBT is based on an educational model.**

CBT is based on the scientifically supported assumption that most emotional and behavioral reactions are learned. Therefore, the goal of therapy is to help clients *unlearn* their unwanted reactions and to learn a new way of reacting.

Therefore, CBT has nothing to do with "just talking." People can "just talk" with anyone. The educational emphasis of CBT has an additional benefit — it leads to long term results. When people understand **how and why** they are doing well, they know what to do to continue doing well.

9. **CBT theory and techniques rely on the Inductive Method.**

A central aspect of *rational* thinking is that it is based on *fact*. Often, we upset ourselves about things when, in fact, the situation isn't like we think it is. If we knew that, we would not waste our time upsetting ourselves.

Therefore, the Inductive Method encourages us to look at our thoughts as being hypotheses or guesses that can be questioned and tested. If we find that our hypotheses are incorrect (because we have new information), then we can change our thinking to be in line with how the situation really is.

10. **Homework is a central feature of CBT.**

If when you attempted to learn your multiplication tables you spent only one hour per week studying them, you might still be wondering what 5 X 5 equals. You very likely spent a great deal of time at home studying your multiplication tables, maybe with flashcards. The same is the case with psychotherapy. Goal achievement (if obtained) could take a very long time if all a person were only to think about the techniques and topics taught was for one hour per week. That's why CBT therapists assign reading assignments and encourage their clients to practice the techniques learned.

## What is Cognitive Behavioral Therapy?[5]

Cognitive behavioral therapy (CBT) is a form of psychological treatment that has been demonstrated to be effective for a range of problems including depression, anxiety disorders, alcohol and drug use problems, marital problems, eating disorders and severe mental illness. Numerous research studies suggest that CBT leads to significant improvement in functioning and quality of life. In many studies, CBT has been demonstrated to be as effective as, or more effective than, other forms of psychological therapy or psychiatric medications. It is important to emphasize that advances in CBT have been made on the basis of both research and clinical practice. Indeed, CBT is an approach for which there is ample scientific evidence that the methods that have been developed actually produce change. In this manner, CBT differs from many other forms of psychological treatment. CBT is based on several core principles, including:

1. Psychological problems are based, in part, on faulty or unhelpful ways of thinking.
2. Psychological problems are based, in part, on learned patterns of unhelpful behavior.
3. People suffering from psychological problems can learn better ways of coping with them, thereby relieving their symptoms and becoming more effective in their lives.

CBT treatment usually involves efforts to change thinking patterns. These strategies might include:

Learning to recognize one's distortions in thinking that are creating problems, and then to reevaluate them in light of reality.

Gaining a better understanding of the behavior and motivation of others.

Using problem-solving skills to cope with difficult situations.

---

[5] The following source: APA Div. 12 (Society of Clinical Psychology) has given their consent to use their description of "What is CBT?"

Learning to develop a greater sense of confidence is one's own abilities.

CBT treatment also usually involves efforts to change behavioral patterns. These strategies might include:

Facing one's fears instead of avoiding them.

Using role playing to prepare for potentially problematic interactions with others.

Learning to calm one's mind and relax one's body.

Not all CBT will use all of these strategies. Rather, the psychologist and patient / client work together, in a collaborative fashion, to develop an understanding of the problem and to develop a treatment strategy.

CBT places an emphasis on helping individuals learn to be their own therapists. Through exercises in the session as well as "homework" exercises outside of sessions, patients / clients are helped to develop coping skills, whereby they can learn to change their own thinking, problematic emotions and behavior.

CBT therapists emphasize what is going on in the person's current life, rather than what has led up to their difficulties. A certain amount of information about one's history is needed, but the focus is primarily on moving forward in time to develop more effective ways of coping with life.

# COMPARISON OF COGNITIVE BEHAVIORAL THERAPY (CBT) AND THE RECOVERY METHOD (RM)

*Note:* The ten points used to describe **CBT** were taken from the full report of the National Association of Cognitive-Behavioral Therapists that is listed in the previous chapter. **RM** (Recovery Method) signifies the author's interpretation of Dr. Abraham Low's Recovery Method, which depicts the similarities to Cognitive Behavioral Therapy.

1. CBT is based on the Cognitive Model of Emotional Response.

Cognitive-behavioral therapy is based on the idea that our *thoughts* cause our feelings and behaviors, not external things, like people, situations and events. The benefit of this fact is that we can change the way we think to feel / act better even if the situation does not change.

**RM.** The Recovery Method teaches that thoughts usually start out as being subjective, perhaps causing the patient to misinterpret what these thoughts mean. If danger is attached to these thoughts, nervous symptoms can develop and, when they do, the patient then begins attaching danger to the symptoms, which can bring on panic attacks. Trained in RM, the patient learns to be more objective in his thinking process and, in most cases, rules out the danger, thus avoiding nervous symptoms. If some symptoms do appear, the patient knows that they, too, are distressing but not dangerous.

2. **CBT is briefer and time-limited.**

Cognitive-behavioral therapy is considered among the most rapid modes in terms of results obtained. The average number of sessions clients receive (across all types of problems and approaches to CBT) is only 16. Other forms of therapy, like psychoanalysis, can take years. What enables CBT to be briefer are its highly instructive nature and the fact that it makes use of homework assignments. CBT is time-limited, in that we help clients understand at the very beginning of the therapy process that there will be a point when the formal therapy will end. The curtailment of the formal therapy is a decision made by the therapist and client. Therefore, CBT is not an open-ended, never-ending process.

**RM.** The Recovery Method is utilized and administered by its members within a weekly self-help community meeting room. The Recovery Method, founded by neuropsychiatrist Dr. Abraham Low, and its meetings are structured and administered by veteran members who have undergone extensive leadership training and been authorized by the Recovery International organization. There is no limit on the amount of meetings anyone wishes to attend. The meetings are free with the option of making a donation. Members are asked to purchase a book written by Dr. Low entitled "Mental Health Through Will-Training" or go to their local library to obtain one. New members are recommended by the Group Leader to attend at least several meetings before they make any decision whether to continue. Many members begin feeling relief within weeks or months but they are told it is up to them on how long they continue attending. There is no time limit. However, they are told to at least stay close to the Recovery Method and not to take it for granted. They are urged to continue to read and reread the main text or some other books by Dr. Low. Attending meetings helps to maintain one's mental health, just as a gym membership aids one's physical health. Taking on leadership assists oneself and others, as well.

3. **A sound therapeutic relationship is necessary for effective therapy, but not the focus.**

Some forms of therapy assume that the main reason people get better is because of the positive relationship between the therapist and client. Cognitive- behavioral therapists believe it is important to have a good, trusting relationship, but that is not enough. CBT therapists believe that the clients change because they learn how to think differently and they act on that learning. Therefore, CBT therapists focus on teaching rational self-counseling skills.

**RM.** The same holds true with Recovery members who have positive relationships with other members. However, it's what they have learned and, above all, have continually practiced using the Recovery Method.

4. **CBT is a collaborative effort between the therapist and the client.**

Cognitive-behavioral therapists seek to learn what their clients want out of life (their goals) and then help their clients achieve those goals. The therapist's role is to listen, teach and encourage, while the client's role is to express concerns, learn, and implement that learning.

**RM.** The Recovery Method is somewhat different with the exception of the final goal that is achieved. In a therapeutic relationship, there's a live professional helping the patient. At a Recovery meeting there is no professional; there are only Recovery peers helping each other with the Method they have learned from each other, which was originated by Dr. Abraham Low. At a Recovery meeting, members give an example of a situation that worked them up, pinpointing what nervous symptoms emerged, and their thoughts or racing thoughts. Next, they apply learned cognitive Recovery tools (known as "spottings") to their situation. Finally, the example giver shares how his situation would have been different before he had received Recovery training. The process highlights all the gains that have been made since using the Recovery Method. Following the given example, the rest of the members offer further spottings that can help even more. The difference here, as compared to the traditional client-therapist model, is that the peers help each other with what they have learned from Dr. Low's Recovery Method. Low is the professional.[6] The essential goal is the mental health of all members.

5. **CBT is based on aspects of stoic philosophy.**

Not all approaches to CBT emphasize stoicism. Rational Emotive Behavior Therapy, Rational Behavior Therapy, and Rational Living Therapy emphasize aspects of stoicism. Beck's Cognitive Therapy is not based on stoicism. Cognitive-behavioral therapy does not tell people how they should feel. However, most people seeking therapy do not want to feel the way they have been feeling. The approaches that emphasize stoicism teach the benefits of feeling, at worst, *calm* when confronted with undesirable situations. They also emphasize the fact that we have our undesirable situations whether we are upset about them or not. If we are upset about our problems, we have two problems — the problem, and our reaction to it. Most people want to have the fewest number of problems possible. So when we learn how to more calmly accept a personal problem, not only do we feel better, but we usually put ourselves in a better position to make use of our intelligence, knowledge, energy and resources to resolve the problem.

**RM.** The Recovery Method would most likely refer to the above

---

[6] Recovery leaders and members are not professionals. Therefore, Dr. Low set forth rules to abide by such as not giving advice, as a professional would do. Medication, religion, politics, sex, medical conditions, giving diagnoses or prognoses, and major events cannot be discussed.

as, "Expect frustrations and disappointments every minute of the day and you won't be as frustrated or disappointed." RM teaches the patient to be a realist. "Realism thrives on logic and reason and romanticism dies of it." Most frustrations and disappointments are going to be trivialities and not major events. Dr. Low would emphasize to his patients that major events happen rarely, but the trivialities of everyday life happen many times a day. It's going to happen, and the patient is not going to get away from it. When the patient learns and practices the Recovery Method, he will see the difference it's going to make in his daily life.

6. **CBT uses the Socratic Method.**

Cognitive-behavioral therapists want to gain a very good understanding of their clients' concerns. That's why they often ask *questions*. They also encourage their clients to ask questions of themselves, like, "How do I really know that those people are laughing at me? Could they be laughing about something else?"

RM. The Recovery Method generally applies to all the members in the group. However, there may be certain situations that bother an individual more than others. These are referred to as "strong links." One patient's strong link may differ from another patient's. After some time, peers get to know each other's strong links. They can point out that, "That's a strong link for Jane and she can chip away at her strong link and attack her weak links." Members can ask questions on the examples that were given so as to better enhance their understanding.

7. **CBT is structured and directive.**

Cognitive-behavioral therapists have a specific agenda for each session, wherein specific techniques / concepts are taught. CBT focuses on the client's goals. We do not tell our clients what their goals "should" be, or what they "should" tolerate. We are directive in the sense that we show our clients how to think and behave in ways to obtain what they want. Therefore, CBT therapists do not tell their clients *what* to do — rather, they teach their clients *how* to do.

**RM.** In the Recovery Method, "knowledge teaches a patient what to do and practice tells him how to do it." This is similar to the above. At Recovery meetings, peers read a chapter of one of Dr. Low's three works: "Mental Health Through Will-Training" (the main text), "Manage Your Fears, Manage Your Anger," and "Selections From Dr. Low's Works." The readings from these books highlight the techniques and concepts of the Recovery Method.

8. **CBT is based on an educational model.**

CBT is based on the scientifically supported assumption that most emotional and behavioral reactions are learned. Therefore, the goal of therapy is to help clients *unlearn* their unwanted reactions and to learn a new way of reacting. And so, CBT has nothing to do with "just talking." People can "just talk" with anyone. The educational emphasis of CBT has an additional benefit — it leads to long-term results. When people understand **how and why** they are doing well, they know what to do to continue doing well.

**RM.** The Recovery Method is similar. When newcomers attend a group meeting, they are bringing with them their old habits that led them into distorted thinking. In Recovery the patients are taught to rid themselves of these old habits that got them to the point of feeling helpless and even hopeless. Dr. Low's writings emphasize "We are not responsible for the illness. It was fate-appointed, not self-inflicted." He goes on to say, "However, once we have been taught what to do, we are now responsible for getting well."

9. **CBT theory and techniques rely on the Inductive Method.**

A central aspect of *rational* thinking is that it is based on *fact*. Often, we upset ourselves about things when, in fact, the situation isn't like we think it is. If we knew that, we would not waste our time upsetting ourselves. Therefore, the inductive method encourages us to look at our thoughts as being hypotheses or guesses that can be questioned and tested. If we find that our hypotheses are incorrect (because we have new information), then we can change our thinking to be in line with how the situation really is.

**RM.** The Recovery Method works in somewhat of the same way. Experiencing a symptom, one may conclude automatically what it means or seems to mean, and then convince himself undeniably. This kind of thinking can make one feel even worse. Recovery teaches that "feeling are not facts; they lie and deceive us and tell us of danger where there is none." Feelings *are* actually felt. The big difference is that they are subjective facts. Jane is feeling a bit of pressure in the chest area and she's wondering what it might be. She begins thinking that it may be indigestion, blood pressure, her nerves or, worse, a heart attack. It *can* be serious. However, all Recovery members are instructed to consult a physician at the outset. Nervous symptoms may appear when a patient might be fearing something or may simply arise out of the blue. The body is actually feeling the pain or discomfort. It is not one's imagination; it is really felt. A physician can explain these subjective feelings in more detail. In most cases, they turn out to be nervous symptoms, which are merely distressing but not dangerous. Now the patient is better informed and becomes more knowledgeable on whether the symptoms are of a nervous origin or something that may be a cause for concern.

10. **Homework is a central feature of CBT.**

If, when one attempts to learn his multiplication tables, he spent only one hour per week studying them, he might still be wondering what 5 X 5 equals. He very likely spends a great deal of time at home studying his multiplication tables, maybe with flashcards. The same is the case with psychotherapy. Goal achievement (if obtained) could be very protracted if a person were to think about the techniques and topics taught for only one hour per week. That's why CBT therapists administer reading assignments and encourage their clients to practice the techniques learned.

**RM.** The Recovery Method works in very much the same way. At Recovery meetings the leader and its members work on encouraging each other to attend their weekly meetings. They are also reminded to read and reread Dr. Low's books and not store them away to be left forgotten. If the patient really wants to get well, he is going to have to make the effort and, when he does, he should always endorse himself and not take it for granted.

# WHO THOUGHT OF CBT AND HOW DID IT ORIGINATE?[7]

Two of the most well-known practitioners who played a part in developing Cognitive Behavioral Therapy are Aaron Temkin Beck and Albert Ellis. One other psychiatrist, not so well known, who I and many others believe pioneered CBT, is Dr. Abraham Low.

**Aaron Temkin Beck**

**Aaron Beck** was born to Russian Jewish immigrants on July 18, 1921 in Providence, Rhode Island, USA, the youngest child of four siblings.

As an American psychiatrist and a Professor Emeritus in the department of psychiatry at the University of Pennsylvania, he is regarded as the father of cognitive therapy, and his pioneering theories are widely used in the treatment of clinical depression. Beck

---

[7] Content cited in this chapter was taken primarily from the *Wikipedia* website. Consent was also obtained from the *Beck Institute for Cognitive Behavior Therapy* to cite any intellectual property contained herein

is noted for his research in psychotherapy, psychopathology, suicide, and psychometrics, which led to his creation of cognitive therapy and the BDI, one of the most widely used instruments for measuring depression severity. Beck is the President Emeritus of the non-profit Beck Institute for Cognitive Behavior Therapy and the Honorary President of the Academy of Cognitive Therapy, which certifies qualified cognitive therapists.

Beck developed cognitive therapy in the early **1960s** as a psychiatrist at Penn. Working with depressed patients, he found that they experienced streams of "negative thoughts" that seemed to pop up spontaneously. He termed these cognitions "automatic thoughts," and discovered that their content fell into three categories: negative ideas about themselves, the world, and the future. Limited time spent reflecting on automatic thoughts would lead patients to treat them as valid.

Beck began helping patients identify and evaluate these thoughts and found that by doing so, patients were able to think more realistically, which led them to feel better emotionally and behave more functionally. He discovered key ideas in CBT, explaining that different disorders were associated with different types of distorted thinking. Distorted thinking has a negative effect on our behavior no matter what type of disorder, he found. Beck explained that successful interventions will educate a person to understand and become aware of his distorted thinking, and how to challenge its effects. He discovered that frequent negative automatic thoughts reveal a person's core beliefs. He explained that core beliefs are formed over lifelong experiences: we "feel" these beliefs to be true.

Since that time, Beck and his colleagues worldwide have researched the efficacy of this form of psychotherapy in treating a wide variety of disorders including depression, bipolar disorder, eating disorders, drug abuse, anxiety disorders, personality disorders, and many medical conditions with psychological components. Cognitive therapy has also been applied with success to individuals with anxiety disorders, schizophrenia, and many other medical and psychiatric disorders. Some of Beck's most recent work has focused on cognitive therapy for schizophrenia, borderline personality disorder, and for patients who are repeat suicide attempters.

Beck has been named one of the "Americans in history who shaped the face of American Psychiatry," and one of the "five most influential psychotherapists of all time" by The American Psychologist in July 1989.

## Albert Ellis

**Albert Ellis** (September 27, 1913 – July 24, 2007) was an American psychologist who, in 1955, developed Rational Emotive Behavior Therapy (REBT). He held M.A. and Ph.D. degrees in clinical psychology from Columbia University and the American Board of Professional Psychology (ABPP). He also founded and was the President for decades of the New York City-based Albert Ellis Institute. He is generally considered to be one of the originators of the cognitive revolutionary paradigm shift in psychotherapy and the founder of cognitive-behavioral therapies. Based on a 1982 professional survey of USA and Canadian psychologists, he was considered the second most influential psychotherapist in history (Carl Rogers ranked first in the survey; Sigmund Freud was ranked third).

In *1947*, Ellis was awarded a Ph.D. in Clinical Psychology at Columbia, and at that time he had come to believe that psychoanalysis was the deepest and most effective form of therapy. However, soon after receiving his Ph.D., Ellis's faith in psychoanalysis was gradually crumbling.

Of psychologists, Ellis credits the writings of Alfred Korzybski, his book, *Science and Sanity*, and general semantics for starting him on the philosophical path for founding rational therapy. In addition, modern and ancient philosophy and his own experiences heavily influenced his new theoretical developments to psychotherapy.

From the late 1940s onward, Ellis worked on REBT and, by January 1953, his break with psychoanalysis was complete, and he began calling himself a rational therapist. Ellis was now advocating a new, more active and directive type of psychotherapy. In 1955, he presented Rational Therapy (RT). In RT, the therapist sought to help the client understand — and act on the understanding — that his personal philosophy contained beliefs that contributed to his own emotional pain. This new approach stressed actively working to change a client's self-defeating beliefs and behaviors by demonstrating their irrationality, self-defeatism and rigidity. Ellis believed that through rational analysis and cognitive reconstruction, people could understand their self-defeatingness in light of their core irrational beliefs and then develop more rational constructs.

In *1954*, Ellis began teaching his new techniques to other therapists and, by 1957, he formally set forth the first cognitive behavior therapy by proposing that therapists help people adjust their thinking and behavior as the treatment for emotional and behavioral problems. Two years later, Ellis published *How to Live with a Neurotic*, which elaborated on his new method.

Despite the relative slow adoption of his approach in the beginning, Ellis founded his own institute. The Institute for Rational Living was founded as a non-profit organization in 1959. By 1968, it was chartered by the New York State Board of Regents as a training institute and psychological clinic.

While many of his ideas were criticized during the 1950s and '60s by the psychotherapeutic establishment, his reputation grew immensely in the subsequent decades. From the 1960s on, his prominence was steadily growing as the cognitive behavioral therapies (CBT) were gaining further theoretical and scientific ground. From then, CBT gradually became one of the most popular systems of psychotherapy in many countries. Ellis had such an impact that in a 1982 survey, American and Canadian clinical psychologists and counselors ranked him ahead of Freud when asked to name the figure who had exerted the average influence on their field. Also in 1982, in an analysis of psychology journals published in the US, it was found that Ellis was the most cited author after 1957. In 1985, the APA presented Dr. Ellis with its award for "distinguished professional contributions."

In the mid-1990s, he renamed his psychotherapy and behavior change system Rational Emotive Behavior Therapy. (It was originally known as Rational Therapy and then Rational-Emotive Therapy.) This he did to stress the interrelated importance of cognition, emotion and behavior in his therapeutic approach. In 1994, he also updated and revised his original 1962 classic book, *Reason and Emotion in Psychotherapy*. During the remainder of his life, he continued developing the theory that cognition, emotion and behavior are intertwined, and that a system for psychotherapy and behavior change must involve all three.

Albert Ellis was such a figure, known inside and outside of psychology for his astounding originality, his provocative ideas, and his provocative personality. He bestrode the practice of psychotherapy like a colossus.

In the opening ceremony of the 2013 American Psychological Association Convention, Ellis was posthumously awarded the APA Award for Outstanding Lifetime Contributions to Psychology. It highlights the profound and historic role played in the life and evolution of the fields of psychology and psychotherapy.

**Abraham Low**

Abraham Low (1891–1954) was a Jewish-American neuropsychiatrist noted for his work establishing self-help programs for the mentally ill. He was born February 28, 1891 in Baranów Sandomierski, Poland and attended grade school, high school and medical school in France from 1910 to 1918. He continued his medical education in Austria, serving in the Medical Corps of the Austrian Army. He graduated with a medical degree in 1919, after his military service, from the University of Vienna Medical School. After serving an internship in Vienna, Austria from 1919 to 1920, Low immigrated to the United States, obtaining his U.S. citizenship in 1927. From 1921 to 1925 he practiced medicine in both New York, New York and Chicago, Illinois. In 1925 he was appointed as an instructor of neurology at the University of Illinois Medical

School and became an associate professor of psychiatry. In 1931 Low was appointed Assistant Director and in 1940 became Acting Director of the University's Neuropsychiatric Institute.

From 1931 to 1941 he supervised the Illinois state hospitals, conducting demanding seminars with the staff and interviewing the most severe mental patients in the wards. In 1936, Low's *Studies in Infant Speech and Thought* was published by the University of Illinois Press. Some sixty papers are by Low dealing variously with such topics as: histopathology of brain and spinal cord, studies on speech disturbances (aphasias) in brain lesions, clinical testing of psychiatric and neurological conditions, studies in shock treatment, laboratory investigations of mental diseases, and several articles on group psychotherapy which had been published in medical periodicals.

In *1937*, Low founded Recovery, Inc. He served as its medical director from 1937 to 1954, during which time he presented lectures to relatives of former patients on his work with these patients and the before and after scenarios. In 1941, Recovery Inc. became an independent organization. Low's three volumes of *The Technique of Self-help in Psychiatric Aftercare* (including "Lectures to Relatives of Former Patients") were published by Recovery, Inc. in 1943. Recovery's main text, *Mental Health Through Will-Training*, was originally published in 1950.

In 1954 Low died at the Mayo Clinic in Rochester, Minnesota. His contributions to the psychiatric and mental health communities are often not well known, but his work has assisted and continues to assist numerous individuals in the area of mental health.

During the organization's annual meeting in June 2007, it was announced that Recovery, Inc. would thereafter be known as Recovery International.

**More on CBT**

CBT was primarily developed through an integration of behavior therapy (first popularized by Edward Thorndike) with cognitive therapy (developed by Aaron Beck and Albert Ellis). While rooted in rather different theories, these two traditions found common ground in focusing on the "here and now" and on alleviating symptoms. I find it astonishing that Dr. Abraham Low's name is not included among Beck's and Ellis's, especially considering that his Method was developed many years before theirs. Low's Method also focuses on the present and the alleviation of symptoms.

CBT is used in both individual and group settings, and the techniques are often adapted for self-help applications.

**Depression**

Cognitive behavioral therapy has been shown as an effective treatment for clinical depression. The American Psychiatric Association Practice Guidelines (April 2000) indicated that, among psychotherapeutic approaches, cognitive behavioral therapy and interpersonal psychotherapy had the best-documented efficacy for treatment of major depressive disorder. One etiological theory of depression is Aaron T. Beck's cognitive theory of depression. His theory states that depressed people think the way they do because their thinking is biased toward negative interpretations. According to this theory, depressed people acquire a negative schema of the world in childhood and adolescence as an effect of stressful life events, and the negative schema is activated later in life when the person encounters similar situations.

Beck also describes a negative cognitive triad, made up of the negative schemata and cognitive biases of the person, theorizing that depressed individuals make negative evaluations of themselves, the world, and the future. Depressed people, according to this theory, have views such as, "I never do a good job," "It is impossible to have a good day," and "Things will never get better." A negative schema helps give rise to the cognitive bias, and the cognitive bias helps fuel the negative schema. This is the negative triad. Beck further proposed that depressed people often have the following cognitive biases: arbitrary inference, selective abstraction, over-generalization, magnification, and minimization. These cognitive biases are quick to make negative, generalized, and personal inferences of the self, thus fueling the negative schema.

**Behavior therapy roots**

Precursors of certain fundamental aspects of CBT have been identified in various ancient philosophical traditions, particularly Stoicism. For example, Aaron T. Beck's original treatment manual for depression states, "The philosophical origins of cognitive therapy can be traced back the Stoic philosophers." The modern roots of CBT can be traced to the development of behavior therapy in the early 20th century, the development of cognitive therapy in the 1960s, and the subsequent merging of the two. Behaviorally-centered therapeutic approaches appear as early as 1924 with Mary Cover Jones' work on the unlearning of fears in children. In 1937, American psychiatrist Abraham Low developed cognitive training techniques for patients' after-care following psychiatric hospitalization.

It was during the period 1950 to 1970 that behavioral therapy became widely utilized by researchers in the United States, the United Kingdom and South Africa, who were inspired by the behaviorist learning theory of Ivan Pavlov, John B. Watson, and Clark L. Hull. In Britain, this work was mostly focused on the neurotic disorders through the work of Joseph Wolpe, who applied the findings of animal experiments to his method of systematic desensitization, the precursor to today's fear reduction techniques. British psychologist Hans Eysenck, inspired by the writings of Karl Popper, criticized psychoanalysis in arguing that "if you get rid of the systems, you get rid of the neurosis," and presented behavior therapy as a constructive alternative. In the United States, psychologists were applying the radical behaviorism of B.F. Skinner to clinical use. Much of this work was concentrated on severe chronic psychiatric disorders, such as psychotic behavior and autism.

## Other roots

Although the early behavioral approaches were successful in many of the neurotic disorders, they had little success in treating depression. Behaviorism was also losing in popularity due to the so-called "cognitive revolution." The therapeutic approaches of Albert Ellis and Aaron Beck gained popularity among behavior therapists, despite the earlier behaviorist rejection of "mentalist" concepts like thoughts and cognitions. Both of these systems included behavioral elements and interventions and primarily concentrated on problems in the present. Albert Ellis's system, originated in the early 1950s, was first called rational therapy, and can (arguably) be called one of the first forms of cognitive behavioral therapy. It was partly founded as a reaction against popular psychotherapeutic theories at the time (mainly psychoanalysis). Beck, inspired by Ellis, developed cognitive therapy in the 1960s. Beck describes his therapeutic approach as originating in a realization he made while conducting free association with patients in the context of classical psychoanalysis. He noted that patients had not been reporting certain thoughts at the fringe of consciousness – thoughts which often preceded intense emotional reaction. This realization led Beck to begin viewing emotional reactions as resulting from *cognitions,* rather than understanding emotion within the abstract psychoanalytic framework. He named these cognitions "automatic thoughts" because he believed that people were not necessarily aware that the cognition existed, but that they could identify these types of thoughts when questioned closely. Beck believed that pushing his clients to identify these automatic thoughts was integral to overcoming a particular difficulty.

In initial studies, cognitive therapy was often contrasted with behavioral treatments to see which was most effective. During the 1980s and 1990s, cognitive and behavioral techniques were merged into cognitive behavioral therapy. Pivotal to this merging was the successful development of treatment for panic disorders.

Starting in the late 1950s and continuing through the 1970s, concurrently with the contributions of Ellis and Beck, Arnold A.

Lazarus developed what was arguably the first form of "broad-spectrum" cognitive behavioral therapy. He later broadened the focus of behavioral treatment to incorporate cognitive aspects. Lazarus, seeking to optimize the efficacy of therapy and effect durable treatment using cognitive and behavioral methods, developed a new form of therapy called multimodal therapy, based on CBT, but also including interpersonal relationships, biological factors, physical sensations (as distinct from emotional states), and visual images (as distinct from language-based thinking).

**Summary**

Of the three professionals highlighted herein who were rooted in Freud's psychoanalysis and who then developed their own forms of psychotherapy (which in time came to be known as "Cognitive Behavioral Therapy"), two received the notoriety and recognition as being the founders of CBT. Ellis was cited in 1954 and Beck in the 1960s. However, in *1937*, American psychiatrist Abraham Low developed cognitive training techniques for patient after-care following psychiatric hospitalization. Additionally, the behaviorally-centered therapeutic approaches of Mary Cover Jones appeared as early as 1924 with her work on the unlearning of fears in children.

Writing from my own knowledge and that which I have read and researched, it was Low who applied both cognitive and behavioral therapy. Patients who were taught by Low then passed his techniques on to other patients. It was years later that prominent professionals such as Beck, Ellis, Wolfe, Lazarus, etc. seemed to be credited as the founding fathers of CBT. Perhaps these prominent professionals gained their knowledge from Dr. Low's works. Regardless, it should be obvious to conclude that it was Dr. Low who pioneered and ushered in Cognitive Behavioral Therapy, referring to it as "changing your thoughts and moving your muscles," later known as "The Recovery Method."

# CHAPTER 15

# DISCUSSIONS ON MENTAL HEALTH TOPICS FROM THE CBT NETWORKING FOR PROFESSIONAL THERAPISTS WEBSITE[8]

Note: This chapter presents opinions from professionals in the mental health field. Along with the professional opinions, there is mine and I'm not a professional. However, since joining Recovery International (RI) self-help mental health organization in 1990 as a nervous patient, I received extensive training in Dr. Abraham Low's Recovery Method and was able to help pass it on to other patients such as myself. After several years I felt qualified to use the knowledge I acquired from RI on the LinkedIn website "CBT Networking for Professional Therapists." I stuck to what I had learned (the Recovery Method) and didn't venture into other areas that only qualified professionals were licensed to do. I joined in many discussions and realized I was receiving quite a bit of respect from these professionals. They agreed and replied in favorable ways, and many of them thanked me and wanted to know even more about the Recovery Method and Dr. Low. I was always happy to tell them, to say the least. I

---

[8] Discussions, held on the LinkedIn website, "CBT Networking for Professional Therapists," are edited and unedited.

*thought, "What a good way to get the word out on who we are and what we know." Highlighting these discussions isn't so much for self-appeasement or self aggrandizement on my part. It's there to show how good Dr. Low's Recovery Method really is. And I'm hoping other veteran RI members will see this and know that they, too, can do the same as I and get the word out, which will help more people receive the help they truly need.*

Discussion:

Exceptionality

Here's a discussion about a patient who wasn't receiving approval from someone she knew and wanted to know how she could deal with it and not let it bother her.

Author:

I believe that what she is experiencing is a case of exceptionality, a term that is used in the Recovery Method (RM). The RM focuses on averageness. Any more or less than the middle road of averageness would be approaching the extremes (too much, too little). What I think this person could achieve is to work on aiming toward that middle road of averageness. The average person would also want no one to upset him. The difference, though, is that the average person would not take it to the extreme and invariably deem it as a bit of frustration or some slight disappointment. If she can focus more on her own inner approval rather than seeking it from others, she would be accomplishing something more important. The Recovery Method stresses that one inner approval is worth more than all outer approvals from others. She can also be taught the difference between "wants" and "needs." In life there are things we all subjectively want that would make us feel good; however, these wants are really not all that important. What is essential, though, is our objective need and that is our mental health. She will have to work on chipping away at her strong link which, of course, is seeking outer approval. She may bear some discomfort (which is not dangerous); however, after practicing this for awhile, she will notice that comfort will come. And lastly, it's important that she endorses herself regardless of how big or small the gain might be rather than take it for granted.

Author's second comment:

Self-appointed expectations lead to self-induced frustrations. We can perpetuate this by constantly seeking outer approval. It is average to seek it, but expecting it is the problem. There's our inner environment and our outer environment. The inner environment consists of our self and everything that transpires within our self. The outer environment is anyone or anything outside ourselves. The things we can't control are the things that are outside our selves short of a bit of influence; however, what we can control is our inner environment. We have a choice: we can work ourselves up, or work ourselves down or just pass it off as a mere frustration. Knowing we can't control outer environment will only help us to understand what and how much are we counting on or expecting from outer environment. Therefore, we should limit ourselves or at least not count on receiving outer approval from others. Learning and understanding this is very important. Applying it is even more so. This lady can also be taught about having her feelings hurt once in awhile. Hurt feelings lead to humility, and humility is the road to inner peace. Everyone is going to have his feelings hurt every now and then, and that is average. Who are we not to have our feelings hurt? If we don't accept this, we will remain in symptoms and continue to practice exceptionality, and exceptionality is a hope, dream and an illusion.

Discussion:

How do you help patients accept uncertainty?

Pamela D., Ph.D., Clinical Psychologist, Life Coach, Author, Speaker[9]

---

[9] Dr. Pamela Darcy is a best-selling author who writes and speaks on leadership attitudes. Email her at info@myinnerguide.com

I want to address the demand for certainty. When you're restructuring the demand for certainty, remember to validate the rational preference behind the demand. So, behind the "I must have certainty" is the healthy desire or rational preference for certainty. It is totally normal to want to have a little certainty in life. For example, you might want to know what's going to happen next and to have a sense of control over your routine. Once you validate that, then move to, "Where we get ourselves into trouble is when we think we must have it," and discuss what are the unfortunate results of that "must" thinking. The other thing to address is the ego anxiety (will I lose face?) and discomfort anxiety (will I be in pain?) that may also be circling around this demand for certainty.

Author:

Certainty or uncertainty brings to mind exceptionality. When a patient feels he must be certain all the time with no allowance for being uncertain, that's a form of exceptionality. The opposite and other extreme, when a patient feels he is always uncertain and beats up on himself, is also a form of exceptionality. Both situations can bring on anxiety and panic. What a patient needs to understand is that there is nothing wrong with being at the middle road of averageness. The acceptance of being certain or uncertain at times can relieve the patient of an unnecessary burden of constantly judging himself, which could initiate anxiety and panic attacks. The standards (or bar) that a patient sets can be too high and when those standards are not met, he begins to panic. I agree with Pamela: "Where we get ourselves into trouble is when we think we must have it." In Dr. Low's works, he discusses wants and needs (patients wanting this and wanting that to the point that they must have it, as Pamela has stated). No matter how strong a feeling is in wanting something desperately, in many cases it is not a need. In giving an example, Low states, "We all need food and water to survive, an objective need; however, garnishing it with spices so that it tastes better is a subjective want."

Discussion:

Right or Wrong

A professional brought up a discussion which had to do with right or wrong and going for symbolic victories. He asked what is the CBT strategy.

Author:

In Low's Recovery Method (which I believe ushered in CBT), he talks about right or wrong as a form of exceptionality (always being right) and uses a phrase: "There are no exceptional people, only exceptional titles." Another phrase is used: "There are no rights or wrongs in the trivialities of everyday life," even in non-trivialities as well. He gives an example such as a judge rendering a decision as to who is guilty (wrong) or not guilty (right). It basically is the judge's opinion of right or wrong. Is your client aware of this righteous arrogance? Whether he is or not, here are a few more phrases from Dr. Low's Method that may help: "Speak with culture, not raw nature;" "Symbolic victories are empty victories;" "Humility is the road to inner peace;" "Peace is for understanding, power for misunderstanding." There are many more concepts on this subject and Dr. Low explains them, so perhaps you may want to learn more.

Professional:

Well said. A judge was a very good example to use. I think Dr. Low's Method is very interesting and I plan to look into it much more and I appreciate you mentioning it.

Author:

I thanked him and said, "Too bad Dr. Low is not as well-known as many other professionals in the mental health field. He certainly should be and probably even more. I usually refer to Low as the one who I believe ushered in CBT and I hope others would look into this as you are doing and see what they think. Low has helped so many people during the 20$^{th}$ century including me, and continues to do so in the 21$^{st}$ century even though he's been deceased since 1954. His Recovery Method might sound old, but it's as good now as it was back then when he had his practice. There's another book that is interesting and was written about him and the Recovery Incorporated (now Recovery International) organization which he created along with his patients. It's called "My Dear Ones," written by Neil and Margaret Rau and it's an excellent read. Enjoy

Professional:

Thank you. I'm deeply into reading Mental Health Through Will Training. It is very enlightening and I very much appreciate it.

Discussion:

Making ourselves RIGHT and others WRONG seems to be one of the principal ego-mind patterns. Any suggestion on how one can consciously change this pattern for a more fulfilling life?

Mike T.L., LMSW, Author, studied at New York University

Author:

Using the late Dr. Abraham Low's Recovery Method (RM) would be a good solution. One of the principles in RM is that there are no rights or wrongs in the trivialities of everyday life. Even in a court of law, they are solely based on opinions of a judge or jury. These right or wrong arguments are referred to in RM as "symbolic victories." And to a person dealing with mental health issues who can't afford the luxury of temper, it becomes an empty victory. There are no winners here, only victims, especially the patient. The thinking usually is, "you gave in," and giving in is a sign of weakness. Contrary to that type of philosophy, it is not a weakness but quite the opposite. The act of lowering your arms and choosing peace over power is far more courageous. When a patient is trained using a try-and-fail-and-try-again method, good mental health is not too far away. To go a step further, this is not to say that one can't express his feelings. He can, but he learns to do so in a more cultured manner. Low uses a helpful phrase: "I am right, you are wrong; lengthen it, deepen it and the sky is the limit on how much one can work himself up."

Lisa F., B.A.; R.P.N, B.A. Psychology, Registered Psychiatric Nurse/ Reproductive Psychiatry Nurse Clinician

Lisa replies:

Thanks, Anthony, for the reference to Dr. Abraham Low's work. I have to plead ignorance and admit I was unfamiliar with him, maybe a reflection of how long I have been away from my psychological roots and academia. I saw an excellent little YouTube clip on some of his work. I like this discussion and hope more people get involved in it. I am going to do some thinking about it and come back for more discussion.

Author:

According to my interpretation of Dr. Low's Recovery Method, I see right and wrong issues placed into two categories: "foreign spotting" and "self-spotting." In most cases, people generally engage mostly in foreign spotting, particularly the client (nervous patient). Foreign spotting consists of seeing the faults of others more readily than one's own, and being quick to make judgments. Alternatively, self-spotting is seldom thought of or practiced upon oneself. If one is willing to change, it's imperative for him to learn the art of self-spotting. Looking into himself and finding his own faults can be difficult, but it can be accomplished. The idea is to find the correct balance. For a client, patient or consumer it's an essential item to learn if one desires to become well and regain his mental health. Maintaining peace, order and balance are key items on the road to recovery.

Mike T. replies:

Thank y'all! Your comments are very helpful. Anthony, thanks for introducing me to Low's Recovery Method, a very stimulating perspective. Being aware by spotting stuff in ourselves and not projecting them onto others is the key.

Discussion:

Anxiety

This discussion is about a patient who is dealing with a medical condition and her worrying about it would set off symptoms. Being aware of it she felt she still could not stop thinking about it. Her professional mentioned to her some relaxation techniques and encouraged her to work on having thoughts that are more realistic.

Author:

I'll start off by saying that I'm not a professional. However, I have received extensive training in Dr. Low's Recovery Method (based in CBT) for 27 years, as a patient, self-help Group Leader, and Area Leader in NYC. It would be helpful to know what your client's medical condition is. Is it serious, or is it something that can be addressed with a little work? In either case, your client can still receive the necessary care. I'll focus on the less serious and leave the other to you professionals.

The word "DANGER" and the words, "There is no danger" are important. Thoughts will come and go as long as we don't attach the idea of danger to them. There are things in life that seem serious when they are merely frustrations and disappointments. Worrying brings on nervous symptoms. Here's where the client needs to know that his symptoms are not "dangerous," they are merely "distressing." How we use words can make situations worse than they are. Replacing the word "worry" with "cause for concern" can help. Here's an important Recovery Method phrase to remember: "There is no thought we cannot change, no impulse we cannot control; feelings and sensations will rise and fall and run their course if we do not attach any danger to them." You mentioned "realistic thoughts." Here's another phrase: "Realism thrives on logic and reasoning; romanticism dies of it." There is plenty on this subject and if you would like to know more, please don't hesitate to contact me here personally, or here on LinkedIn.

Comments:

Three professionals replied back to me in this discussion. One thanked me and agreed with me that language is important. Another mentioned that it was very good advice. The third said that he would like to know more on this subject. He mentioned about semantics being the key and that it's amazing that many therapists seem to ignore it.

Discussion:

Author:

"Physical illness and mental illness. Why is there a separation? Or, is there a separation?"

Kimberly T., Licensed Psychologist:

I am doing my clinical psychology post doc year at a rural ob-gyn clinic. I don't think there is a separation. I approach it from a dynamic systems perspective. I think we are rediscovering old insights into the mind-body connection and adding new ones all the time. If I didn't believe that mind and body work seamlessly together, I don't think

I'd be able to work in this setting. The physicians and midwife refer to me, and I keep an open mind about the usefulness of medication for different problems and collaborate with them so that the patient is able to work on her problems from multiple perspectives.

Comments:

There were a few other professional replies to this question. One felt there was no separation and that the body functions as a unit. Another commented that the body and mind function in unison and are interdependent and that is why diseases are labeled. Yet in another reply, it is stated that physical and mental illnesses are separate. Physical illness can be seen and felt thus making a direct correlation. Mental illness is different. Sometimes it goes unnoticed (no pain, swelling, blood) and other times it is misdiagnosed due to lack of knowledge. Therefore, we identify with physical illnesses as they are manifested (side effects); they have disabling / uncomfortable effects, and require the use of rest and medication to recover. This professional continued on that society still stigmatizes counseling and whether there is a difference is relevant to the beholder. As long as mental illness is not recognized and continues to be stigmatized by society, more people will go unattended and problems will increase. The professional concluded with, "I wonder when society will wake up and invest more into mental health."

Author:

My reason for bringing up this discussion is because of the stigma which society places on mental illness, with phrases such as: "snap out of it" (like a mere snap will alleviate symptoms), "it's all in your head"(like what you're feeling is not real)," and "go to the doctor and get a checkup." The patient does and the doctor says, "I can't find anything wrong with you" or "I can't find anything physically wrong with you." Too many times this paints the wrong picture for the patient, who is thinking, "I'm not making it up, I know what I'm feeling, I'm not crazy."Unfortunately, what doesn't get mentioned on too many occasions is that there really is a pain and sensations in the organs of the body but, because there is, it doesn't mean there is something physically wrong with the organs. We also know there are defects in the brain that cause mental illness. Knowing this, why then is mental illness not placed in the physical illness category, as are ailments affecting other organs? Another interesting item is that recently, mental health treatment costs have finally gained some ground by reaching parity with the likes of other physical ailments. Why did it take so long? Is it stigma again? I believe that mental illness should be placed under the heading of physical illnesses, such as heart disease, lung disease, diabetes, etc.

Discussion:

Not able to focus, gets into thoughts in a conversation and feels bad about himself, does it seem to be ADD? Suggestions appreciated.

Dharani S., College student counselor at Vickram Engineering College & Vickram Polytechnic College Top Contributor

My client is 29 yrs old but has this experience from childhood. He has completed his graduation, he feels bad about not being able to focus more than 15 minutes, he gets absorbed in his own thinking when people communicate, but to my shock he is an assistant professor. He is able to teach for ½ hr but easily gets distracted by disturbance.

Author:

Not being a professional, I will avoid making any kind of diagnosis. Here's an example and some thoughts in relationship to my own tendencies. If someone read a cartoon and laughed and then said to me, "Here, read this, it's pretty funny," I would usually tend to tense up because I would feel I have to read it and laugh, otherwise what would this person think of me if I didn't laugh? Now that this thought came into my head, I would not want to look embarrassed, rather than simply reading it and just letting the chips fall where they might, as most people would do. My anxiety would cause me to have two different thoughts at the same time, whereas the average person might normally have one. These two thoughts would get scrambled and lead to me losing my concentration. Maybe that's what this patient is doing. As an assistant professor he may also be comparing himself with his own peers. It could even extend to his students. What if they asked a question and he didn't have the answer or answered it incorrectly? He may be predisposed to making mistakes or looking foolish. If this happens to apply to this patient, here is what I've learned to overcome these types of situations. I've learned that I placed too much emphasis on seeking outer approval when my own inner approval is much more important. Seeking outer approval is a subjective want, not an objective need. I've learned that I'm a capable person and, rather than paralyzing myself with my own fears, I must have the courage to make mistakes, if they are mistakes, in the trivialities of everyday life; work on having a sense of humor in the quiet realization of my own averageness; learn to bear discomfort and comfort will come; and endorse myself for all of my efforts, not just successes. I hope this applies and helps. However, if it doesn't, I'll endorse myself for all of my efforts anyway.

Discussion:

I have a young man with PTSD, severe explosive tendencies and agoraphobia, social anxiety.

Marc A., Private Psychotherapist, LCW, Top Contributor

Hello, Colleagues. I have a client who has PTSD with moderate social anxiety and agoraphobia. He's a very nice young man in his 20s. He feels highly anxious "95%" of the time, according to the client. Once in awhile, he will get into an explosive situation with someone on the street, a family friend, etc. which the client cannot control. He has zero frustration tolerance in these situations and he describes there being no time between the antecedent trigger and the impulse to act out angrily. He has some insight into this and agrees that it is a fight-or-flight reaction that can be traced back to trauma in high school – abuse from other students. He feels he has to act really tough in those situations, being "from the ghetto," and thinks he has to act aggressively first lest he be attacked. The most imminent problem is the explosion. I want to figure out a way to distance his acting out from the trigger, as there is no time between the two. Also, he gets very uncomfortable in crowds (i.e., supermarket), which makes it hard for him to figure out and take care of things (he doesn't go to school or work), and can't socialize, as people generally make him feel very uncomfortable. Thank you!

Author:

I see what most likely is an exaggerated description of himself. He seems to focus on the extremes. Low's Recovery Method focuses quite a bit on the patient who will tend to speak and react in an extreme manner. Saying he has "zero frustration tolerance," and no time between acting out his impulse, he feels he has to act toughly and aggressively. The words he uses in describing himself and his reactions are extreme (temperamental lingo). In order to get well, he needs to become a realist, working toward being an average person and cutting down on the extremes. By saying he has "zero frustration," he closes the door to having any tolerance at all. What he needs to know is he does have tolerance. It just needs to be cultivated. Other areas that need to be worked on are bearing discomfort, comparisons with others and seeking outer approval. "We get well by the amount of discomfort we're willing to bear;" also, "Bear the discomfort and comfort will come." There are concepts that need to be chipped away at, and when we accomplish it, we should endorse ourselves for it and not take it for granted. Move away from comparing ourselves with others. The only thing we should compare ourselves with is before we got well and after we got well. We all would like to receive approval from others; however, it's really not very important and falls into the category of a want and not a need. What is important, however, is seeking our own inner approval, which is far more important than all the outer approvals we can receive from others.

Marc replies:

Great, useful insights. Thanks very much.

Author:

Just want to add to my first comment. The word "explosive" would be considered "temperamental lingo" according to Low's Recovery Method / CBT. Also highlighted: "which client cannot control." He may feel he lacks control, but he really doesn't; he just needs to practice the training / therapy. "Temper may not always be controlled, but it's not uncontrollable." He has "zero frustration tolerance." Here, again, temperamental lingo is used. He basically feels he has zero frustration tolerance. He has more than he thinks, but he is just not aware of it until now. "No time between" would be considered "the mania for exaggeration" similar to the other items I've pointed out. This is what the patient usually does, but it is not necessarily his fault since he hasn't been taught the concepts as of yet. However, once he is taught, he is then responsible to practice them and get well.

Phyllis G., Recovery International Group Leader and Assistant District Leader of Tampa Bay Area, Florida

Anthony, I enjoyed seeing your posts on this site. They are so effective but people have to be ready to help themselves. Recovery International lets a person see he is not alone. It is much easier to sit in a room with people who are also going through some of the things you are coping with. We retrain the brain to think about things differently. You can find peace within your life using Dr. Low's Method. CBT is the way to go for lots of people out there who do not even know how angry and fearful they are.

Author:

I'd like to focus on one of the items that make the patient very uncomfortable. Your last sentence said he "can't socialize, as people generally make him feel very uncomfortable." I believe Low's Method would describe this as: It's not people that make the patient feel very uncomfortable, it's the patient himself. A patient's predispositions govern his dispositions. The patient needs to understand that he cannot change or control anyone other than himself. He needs to be taught how to deal with these situations. These are mere frustrations and disappointments that are trivial which the patient has experienced over time and made into major events. He feels he has to act out his frustrations when these events happen, but he doesn't. As we learn in RI: "Every action doesn't always require a reaction." If at times one feels he wants to say something, he can do it with culture, not raw nature. In one of Low's lectures a patient asked, "Isn't it better to speak up and get it off your chest rather than holding on to it?" Low replied, "On the contrary, it takes more courage to be calm and not give in to temper and, when the patient does this, he by all means should endorse himself." Additionally, "Choose peace over power," "Peace is for understanding and power is for misunderstanding," "We get well by the amount of discomfort we're willing to bear," and "Calm begets calm and temper begets temper."

We must eliminate or reduce certain lingo such as: "very," "always" or "can't." Substitute: "I care not to" for "can't." I believe I said this earlier in one of my comments. Saying "can't" sort of closes the door or eliminates any attempt to try to improve (get well). It comes down to the patient not wanting to bear discomfort; however, when he is taught and given the tools, he will learn gradually about bearing discomfort. It's a "try-and-fail, try-and-fail-until-you-succeed" method.

Marc replies:

Very helpful. Thanks again. We'll take a look at the word "choices" as well as some of these other aspects.

Discussion:

Temper

A teenager is having anger issues with a female teacher and needs help. He responded well to CBT and is mindful with family and friends. There was a decrease in some of his outbursts, and he has done some work and tries his best. As for school, he needs supervision. He had been on medication and his doctor said he had high testosterone levels, but has been off medication for a period of time. He is quite young compared to others at the same level. He has developed a reputation that is not helping him and needs help in keeping calm with those in authority, especially those who are female. His mother has a strong personality.

Author:

Dr. Low's Recovery Method deals a lot with anger issues. From this description, I get the impression that being younger than other seniors in high school is negative (insecure thinking), when it should, alternatively, be deemed as positive (secure thinking). Being still young and graduating appears to me as something to be proud of. His mother, fellow students and others may say or do things that may upset him and it is average to feel that way. He must learn that he will most likely not be able to change that, since we really can't control what others do or say; we can only hope to influence. However, we can learn and be able to control ourselves so that it won't work us up as much or not at all. If we can't change a situation, we will have to learn to change our attitude. If he complains to others or silently to himself, he will be wise to stop the verbal or muscular habit of complaining, which will then put an end to the mental habit of defeatism. Patients can't afford the luxury of temper. Again, we must learn to express ourselves with culture and not raw nature. Subjective wants and objective needs are two different concepts. We feel we want to shout out something in anger to someone: that's our subjective want. But we will learn that what's really important is our objective need. A patient may want to receive approval from others and that's understandable; however, what's more important is our objective need, which is our inner approval, and worth far more than all the outer approvals we can garner. Keep in mind, every act of self-control leads to a rise in self-respect. There's so much more in Low's Method that is applicable here.

Author's second comment:

I have found, being a nervous patient to nervous person, then as a Group Leader and, later on, as Area leader for New York City in RI, how important it is to learn about dealing with temper. I had no idea how important it was. I experienced anxiety that brought on panic attacks and depression. What did temper have to do with it? I learned it had plenty to do with it. Dr. Low's Method gave me the tools to use and I used them well, but maybe not all the time. I did sabotage now and then, but found out that was average as long as we didn't give up. Low gave us a spotting (a phrase/quote), as it is called: "Sabotage to a minimum and endorse to a maximum." What I learned in RI as a nervous patient and needed to learn can help everyone who tends to jump to conclusions too quickly. Seeking excitement in devious ways brings on the excitement. When someone acts, we don't always have to react. We must be patient and take a "wait and see attitude." If one feels he needs to act, do it in a cultured manner. "Feelings call for expression, and temper for suppression or control."

Author's third comment:

I know quite a bit about Dr. Abraham Low, the creator of the Recovery Method and founder of Recovery International (RI). Much of Low's writings had to do with temper. Low describes temper as having two forms: angry and fearful. Angry temper is directed toward anyone and anything other than the patient himself. Fearful temper is directed toward the patient himself. Angry temper consists of having resentment and indignation, while fearful temper consists of being ashamed, embarrassed, having low self-esteem, etc. These tempers bring on symptoms which fan the flames of temper even further. To overcome both these types of temper, Low instructs that the patient will have to be trained on how to manage and bring them under reasonable control. Dropping the judgment against others and one's own self will have to be employed to a maximum. Avoid going for symbolic victories which will only bring on empty victories. Patients with an abundance of temper need to be told that they can't afford the luxury of temper, just like the diabetic who can't afford the luxury of eating certain foods. In several books and writings and in the creation of his Recovery Method, Low focused extensively on how temper plays a very important role in maintaining a patient's mental health. It can be difficult at times working on convincing the patient that "yes," it may be someone else's fault that makes him angry at times; however, looking for someone else to blame or change the patient's disposition is not realistic and, in almost all cases, will fail. The patient needs to learn he can't control what others may do or say and holding on to judgment of them will only prolong the temper. The patient must learn that it is he who needs to change or adjust to these situations. The therapist, Low and self-help groups can supply the tools for the patient to use while making these adjustments. It is helpful to embrace Dr. Low's adage: "If you can't change a situation, you will have to change your attitude toward it."

Dropping the judgment against others must consist of eliminating, or at least holding to a minimum, both the verbal habit of complaining or silently complaining to oneself. This, by no means, translates into taking the other person off the hook. What it does mean, however, is that we are taking our own self off the hook of not getting all worked up over it, and thereby reducing it to what it most likely is. That's a triviality according to our mental health. Life's frustrations and disappointments consist mainly of trivialities. Major events are rare and few.

Discussion:

Thoughts: Racing thoughts in bipolar disorders

Racing thoughts in bipolar disorders. And what are the CBT techniques that can be used that have been effective in managing them?

Author:

Dr. Abraham Low's Recovery Method and writings would be an excellent reference. In his fundamental book, "Mental Health Through Will-Training," we find a multitude of techniques pertaining to racing thoughts. Thoughts can be intrusive, indeed. But we are not responsible for the quality of our thoughts. Low emphasized the word "DANGER" and how patients tend to attach it to many of their thoughts. There are secure and insecure thoughts, he explains. And of course, the patient focuses too much on the insecure thoughts. For the patient to regain his mental health, he is required to undergo the training of removing most of these insecure thoughts or, at a minimum, removing the danger from them. Low uses phrases such as: "A thought produced it and a thought can take it away" and "Have the thought but don't make an issue of it and it will die of its own inanition." He uses the term "averageness" to be mindful of not going to the extremes of highs and lows but, rather, maintaining the middle road of averageness. Peace, order and balance are what the patient should strive toward.

Discussion:

OCD patients and good exercises for intrusive thoughts (a lot of "should've" feelings)

Author:

I would recommend Dr. Abraham Low's book," Mental Health Through Will-Training" and other works of his. I agree with others whom I've heard speak about intrusive thoughts not being harmful and guiding them so as to not deem them as harmful or just simply changing them. Dr. Low instructs, "Practice objectivity and objectivity will terminate panic." He goes on to explain that practicing objectivity with your thoughts is to focus on items completely unemotional, suggestive or dealing with excitement. The reasoning behind (or my interpretation of) what Low is saying is that these kinds of thoughts can keep one in symptoms even further; however, by practicing objectivity we therefore eliminate all the thrills, excitement and adventure in these thoughts, something detrimental for a patient.

Here are some additional items on intrusive (insecure) thoughts from Dr. Low's Recovery Method:

Insecure thoughts are intruders of the brain, as are burglars or uninvited guests. They come not at our bidding. Have these thoughts and don't make an issue of them and they will die of their own inanition; thoughts will rise and fall and run their course as long as we don't attach the idea of danger to them; a thought produced it and a thought can take it away; and we can work on changing any insecure thoughts to secure thoughts. The essential thing is to practice not attaching any danger to these thoughts. They may be distressing but they are certainly not dangerous. The patient must learn to not process insecure thoughts. By continuing to do so, he will likely remain in symptoms, progressively worsening the situation. Low's RM may seem relatively simple, and it is; however, what is not so simple is practicing it. It's a "try-and-fail, try-and-fail-till-you-succeed" method. And every time we work on it and put it into practice, we endorse ourselves and not take it for granted, for all the effort we put into it. It's the effort that counts most of all and which will eventually lead us to maintaining good mental health.

Discussion:

Where do our "thoughts" come from?

Mike T., LMSW, Author, studied at New York University

This question comes from Eckhart's teachings. I'm hoping that someone may simplify it more or link it to CBT since CBT came into being thanks to dysfunctional "thoughts."

Author:

I suppose certain thoughts may have developed from the kind of environment in which one had grown up. The interesting thing about thoughts is they can come from "out of the blue," any time or any place, whether we want them to or not. In the business of mental health, we are mainly concerned with whether they are secure or insecure thoughts. Either way, they will come. Neuropsychiatrist Abraham Low refers to some of these thoughts as "intruders or buglers of the brain." He says, "They come not at our bidding and we are not responsible for having them;" however, he continues, "We are responsible for entertaining them." He is referring to his patients who have received training in the Recovery Method (CBT, if you may). One of my favorite quotes by Dr. Low is, "There are no thoughts we cannot change, no impulses we cannot control, and symptoms and sensations rise and fall and run their course if we do not attach any danger to them." Here are just a few other profound quotes made by Low in reference to thoughts: "We can change an insecure thought for a secure thought;" "a thought produced it, and a thought can take it away;" "have the thought and don't make an issue of it, and it will die of its own inanition."

Mike T. and 4 others like the above.

Thomas C., Senior Lecturer at London South Bank University:

Thanks for that, Anthony.

Thomas replies:

Thanks Anthony. I am also of the opinion that appraisals are influenced by past experiences, culture, threats that you have alluded to in the last post. I think the content of the thoughts has many influences, but how they are physically manifested or originate is a tough one.

Author:

Mike, perhaps you can clarify the question. Are you asking about what influences thoughts, or how they are physically manifested?

Mike replies:

BOTH, how they are conceived, where, and how they show up.

Author:

Some additional points on insecure thoughts:
In my own experience with nightmares and insecure thoughts, I found the more I feared them, the more they would intensify. When I learned not to attach any danger to these thoughts because that's all they were (just thoughts and not reality), the less they manifested. Occasionally I'll get these thoughts, but I apply the same principles and they die of their own inanition. It can be helpful to remember: "There are no thoughts we cannot change,

and no impulses we cannot control; symptoms and sensations will rise and fall and run their course as long as we don't attach any DANGER to them."

Discussion:

Anxiety: A therapist asked if we can come up with some strategies that can be used for those dealing with anxiety and if we can recommend resources

Author:

I would focus on "exceptionality" (which was also explained in the first discussion). Striving at being perfect is desirable and understandable; however, expecting it to happen all the time is unrealistic. If a person succeeds in accomplishing something exceptionally well that person should by all means endorse himself. If he doesn't succeed or do as well as he had hoped for, he still should endorse himself for making an effort and at times possibly even more than when he is successful. *Effort* needs to be emphasized. It would also be good for him to learn not to constantly look for outer approval, which is a subjective want. More importantly, he should look for his own inner approval, which would be his objective need. Here are a few phrases from Dr. Low's Recovery Method: Exceptionality is a hope, dream and illusion; one inner approval is worth more than all the outer approvals one can receive; realism thrives on logic and reason, romanticism dies of it; have the courage to make a mistake if indeed it is a mistake in the trivialities of everyday life; endorse yourself for all your efforts, not only your successes; subjective wants and objective needs; excuse yourself rather than accuse for the sake of your own mental health; and, lastly, are the nervous symptoms one gets from anxiety and that is: symptoms are distressing but they are not dangerous.

Discussion:

Stigma: This is about a client thinking about whether it's ridiculous to tell her boyfriend that she's dealing with bipolar disorder.

A professional brought out that it depends on the relationship and how long they have been together and how much they know about one another's emotions. It's not something a person would say in the early stages. However, within a reasonable amount of time when they are getting to understand and trust one another, it would most likely be okay to bring out.

Author:

I believe that should be up to each individual. I'd love to see the day when a question such as this would not even be thought of being asked. For now, in the real world, common sense should prevail. As long as stigma exists, it would have to be dealt with. If you've been dating only for a short time, I believe it's okay not to say anything. However, if the relationship becomes more serious, I would then suggest choosing an appropriate time to share it. In any case, if you tell your boyfriend and things go sour after that, I recommend you don't blame yourself. You may be hurt and upset in the short term but, in the long term, it should work out to be better for you.

Professional:

The professional agreed with what I had said and added a bit more by mentioning that if the client got that close to him in the first place, it would be fine to share. In fact, he went on to bring out that if the boyfriend was insightful, he would already know it or have thought something about it, and it might be validating. Why would you have gotten that close to anyone to whom it would not be okay to say that? He felt it depended on the relationship, which may be a copout, although different people do have different levels of closeness.

Discussion:

When fear presents itself as a "sick feeling" in the stomach

Wendy Allonby, CBT student and Senior Occupational Therapist in NHS mental health assessment and treatment

I've just starting working with a man whose life is paralyzed by bouts of extreme fear which present as a 'sick feeling' (but not specified what) which start when he wakes up. He is attempting to avoid these sensations through staying in bed (he also frequently vomits to try to rid himself of the sensations). He has tried acceptance of the physical pain. This doesn't work, and it just intensifies the focus until it becomes unbearable. He has tried every approach (including some unusual ones I haven't come across). There may be scope for some cognitive restructuring (after thought diaries and hot cross buns) as the appraisals are clearly part of what is then creating a low mood and some suicidal ideation. He wants to understand why this happens. There is a history of health anxiety in teenage years, childhood emotional abuse / domestic violence and probably social anxiety. Could you share your thoughts please?

Author:

I suggest you pick up a copy of "Mental Health Through Will-Training" by Dr. Abraham Low. I believe this book will give you a world of knowledge, especially in the area of your client's difficulty. I'll try and give you a brief idea of what Dr. Low talks about in his book. First, let me say Dr. Low wrote several other books and created what is known as the Recovery Method. This Method is used by Recovery International, a self-help mental health organization which he originated. I and many others believe he ushered in CBT. That said, here are a few items that might help you and your client. The sensations your client is feeling in the morning would be considered a nervous symptom which is distressing but not dangerous. The patient actually does feel them. They are not imagined, they are real. The important thing to understand is that these symptoms pose no danger to the client, as long as he is physically checked out by a physician and the findings show no problems to the physical aspects of the body. It's good to know that the opposite of fear is that there is no danger. Symptoms in the morning are most prevalent because the patient sees the whole day before him. Movement of the muscles overcomes defeatism of the brain. Practicing and chipping away, setting small goals in the beginning is what needs to be done. Rather than forcing oneself to rise in the morning and face the day ahead the patient can accomplish it in small parts. Start with one thing in mind at a time: go to the bathroom, and when completed endorse himself (pat on the back). Continue to the $2^{nd}$ and $3^{rd}$ steps. If he doesn't complete all the steps, he should endorse himself anyway for what he at least achieved. He is now proving that by using his muscles he can function in spite of having symptoms. It's try and fail, try and fail till you succeed. By practicing in this manner, the symptoms will eventually diminish and it will soon become apparent that the muscles are the humble educators of the brain. Feelings are not objective facts; they can lie, deceive us and tell us of danger when there is none. There is so much more that can be learned with the Recovery Method. I learned it and it helped me tremendously, which enabled me to go on helping others.

Wendy A. replies:

Anthony, thank you for sharing, Recovery is very much a focus on our team. Similar approaches which fit with your description are behavioral activation (which I am doing). The step-by-step approach is part of graded approach, also described in Kaizen. I will keep your post and look at the reference you suggest.

Charles M., Clinical Psychologist, author[10]

---

[10] Charles Merrett is the author of "The Origins of Anxiety."

I am sure you are right when you say he hasn't found a way of accepting and not being concerned about the sensations. To state the obvious, this also means that he is reacting to them in a strongly negative way, i.e., he is actively doing something. If we understand anxiety as something we are doing (at the time we are actually anxious) in the way we are predicting and not wanting something, what he is doing / thinking each morning is the problem. Of course, at this stage he might not be able to identify the details of what this is. I would suggest that the first step should be to establish a thorough cognitive understanding of anxiety as a natural, necessary human response that comprises both predicting something and not wanting it / being fearful of it. It is important to stress that we can only feel anxious when we are doing / thinking like this. This also means that if the problem is something the person is doing now, the history is less important and focusing on it can lead to self-descriptions that are negative and the idea that the cause is somewhere in the past. I would also suggest not rushing to find a technique before a thorough understanding is established, as this can lead to technique dependence and the idea that the person, at best, can only cope with his anxiety and that he must always be on his guard against it.

Author:

I would like to add another comment. Using logic and reason can help a patient in understanding why he may be having pain at a particular time. A diseased organ can bring on pain and the pain can be felt regardless of the day or time it is. However, if the pain only happens at a particular time or day (in this case it's in the morning), chances are the pain is of a nervous origin. And as most of us have been saying, that pain is real. The difference is it's a subjective feeling by the patient in thinking that the organ may be damaged, when in fact the pain is brought on by attaching danger to whatever he is feeling and thinking about at that time. These insecure thoughts feed the symptoms and the pain becomes stronger and turns into a vicious cycle of helplessness. When the patient is taught that nervous symptoms are distressing but not dangerous, he can then work on turning what was once a vicious cycle of helplessness into a vitalizing cycle of self-confidence.

# CHAPTER 16

# RECOVERY METHOD MENTAL HEALTH TOOLS TO LIVE BY

In this chapter, the individual suffering nervous symptoms will acquire an awareness of how he can help himself just by learning some of the techniques described in this chapter. Knowledge alone will not help. Simply knowing something but not practicing it will be of no help at all. Having the conviction to practice and be willing to bear some discomfort is the key to getting well. And getting well is the result of turning what was once a vicious cycle of helplessness into a vitalizing cycle of self-confidence.

Nervous symptoms and self-diagnosing

Simply put and good to know, "nervous symptoms are distressing but they are not dangerous" (whether the symptoms are stomach distress, head pressure, heart palpitations, difficulty breathing, or whatever else), provided you've been examined by a physician and his findings show that there is nothing physically abnormal that would have brought on the symptoms. It is then when the doctor would usually say something such as, "I can't find anything physically wrong, and so I would conclude that the symptoms were likely brought on by anxiety within the nervous system." Some patients have a difficult time understanding this, and insist that something is physically wrong and seek a second or third opinion and in some cases, many more. Patients may say things such as, "I know what I'm feeling, doctor, how can it be just nerves?" They go on with, "I'm not imagining it, I'm actually feeling it." There are even some people who would risk going for an operation rather than accept the fact that what they are dealing with are nervous symptoms that are indeed treatable.

One must learn to be a realist if he consults a doctor and is given a diagnosis, and then is instructed on what he needs to do to get well. It is important that he follow his physician's directions. Too often patients don't do what the doctor tells them. If the patient feels that the doctor is wrong he can go to another doctor, and many patients do just that. However, when they do consult another doctor they tend to discount that doctor as well. When one seeks treatment from a professional but doesn't necessarily follow directions he is sabotaging the doctor's authority. He is now self-diagnosing and doing what he feels should be done, not what the doctor tells him. Being realistic means to understand that a physician is trained to diagnose and prescribe what needs to be done.

Another form of self-diagnosing is when one feels something is ailing him and he develops a fiery imagination that something terrible is happening. In most cases patients with nervous conditions usually fear the worst. Before seeing a doctor they may ask relatives or friends for advice and God only knows what they may say. Here again, being realistic and using common sense should prevail. Leave the diagnosing to the physician.

Temper

Mental health patients need to learn how to deal with temper. There are two types of temper: angry and fearful. Angry temper is associated with having temper toward anyone or anything outside of one's own self, while fearful temper is the opposite and is directed at one's self.

How can we control temper? We will not be able to control temper fully; however, we can hold it to a minimum where it won't affect our mental health. It would be good to remember that "temper may not always be controlled but it's not uncontrollable." Here's an example of both angry and fearful tempers. You meet a friend you haven't seen in some time and he greets you with, "Hi, I haven't seen you for ages. Where have you been hiding? You don't call or email any longer. Have you forgotten your friends?" With this, angry temper is brought on in the form of resentment, indignation and "How dare he say that. Who does he think he is?" You begin to work yourself up and want to get back at him with something cruel. Or maybe you don't get back with a rude remark and walk away. Now both tempers are working you up, angry because of what he said and fearful because you're angry at yourself for not getting back at him. You feel ashamed, embarrassed, and weak. You are now holding onto a judgment of him (angry temper) and yourself (fearful temper). Scenarios such as this happen to many people and it's not unusual, but when one holds on to judgment time after time, his mental health suffers.

The good news is that one can learn how to deal with everyday situations similar to this example, so that it doesn't bridge into his mental health. How is it done? We learn that these things are average (it happens to others) and not to take them seriously. We don't hold on to judgment continuously; we learn to let go. We can use humor and make it our "best friend" while making temper our "worst enemy." When we learn to laugh at our frustrations, it will then become difficult to take them seriously. We learn we can't control what people say or do, but we can control ourselves not to let it bother us. Thoughts of these frustrations will come into our head, but we learn we are not responsible for having them. However, we are responsible for holding on to them. It is good to remember that "a thought produced it and a thought can take it away." Another sabotaging point is "the complaining habit," and a valuable tool is to learn to "drop the verbal habit of complaining, thereby putting an end to the mental habit of defeatism." One must learn to decrease the amount of complaining, whether it's to others or to ourselves. Symptoms will undoubtedly remain if complaining continues.

Temperamental (extreme) language

If one is to help another, he must be instructed to use language which is not extreme. This is important because language, when used loosely, can be alarming and defeatist. Language frequently brings on tenseness, which reinforces and perpetuates symptoms. Features, gestures and symptoms speak, and to the individual it preaches "DANGER." Because he attaches danger, palpitations now feel violent and bring on the thought of sudden death. The pressure in the head is viewed as a brain tumor. The tenseness he experienced is so terrible he feels he's going to burst. With thoughts and feelings such as these, the patient begins to develop the fear of physical collapse, mental collapse and the permanent handicap.

Language used in an extreme manner by an individual, or hearing it from friends or relatives, sets the stage for temperamental reactions which in turn reinforce symptoms and increases them in intensity. Unthinking attitudes from friends and relatives with coarse statements only add to the individual's agony. Implying that he makes no effort to get well, he is indicted as a weakling and told to "snap out of it," as though it were that simple. The individual, constantly hearing all this, gradually accepts their insinuations, and becomes ashamed and fearful. This is also true of nervous symptoms. By labeling sensations as "intolerable," feelings as "terrible," or impulses as "uncontrollable," the language discourages the individual from facing, tolerating and controlling the reaction. Extreme language, whether spoken, heard or thought of by the individual, prevents him from getting well. He must learn to avoid the extremes of temperamental language.

Learning what we can or cannot control

Basically, we have the capability of controlling ourselves; unfortunately, many of us have a difficult time doing just that.

On the other hand, we seem to think we are capable of controlling others. However, that kind of thinking needs to be turned around and adjusted. At best, we may have some influence, but that's about it. Realistically, it's important that we learn and get it into our heads rather than getting all worked up wishing, hoping and getting angry trying to accomplish it. What is of importance and worth focusing on is gaining the knowledge and even more important, is practicing how to control ourselves. When people or other elements in life cause us to get all worked up we have to understand that's part of life and not to take it too seriously. It's going to happen to others as well. The choice is ours and learning how to deal with it is essential in maintaining our mental health. The longer and stronger we hold on trying to control anything outside ourselves, the longer and stronger our symptoms will be. We have to learn to be average and not make a mountain out of a mole hill. Stop going for symbolic victories, they only become empty victories. Dealing with who is right and who is wrong is really not all that important as we seem to think especially when your mental health is at stake. If your feelings get hurt, so be it. Others get their feelings hurt, why can't we? Getting feelings hurt once in awhile will teach us humility and humility is the road to inner peace. Having everything go the way we want and not having our feelings hurt is a "want" (unimportant and unrealistic) but not a "need" (important and realistic) in maintaining our mental health.

Muscle control

Muscle training may be a little unusual in the technique of learning how to maintain your mental health, but it's really not. A simple way to understand muscle control is when one feels he has to do something he dislikes. Whether it's moving muscles or controlling muscles not to move is the same thing. Doing the things we hate and fear to do is where muscle control comes into play. After learning that symptoms are distressing but not dangerous, the only way to convince oneself that the symptoms are just that is to prove it, simply by performing the act. For example: a person wants to go shopping but fears he or she will go into symptoms on the way there or in the store. Now is the time for the patient to utilize muscle control. A bit apprehensive, he goes and accomplishes his objective. The muscles have now convinced the brain that there was no danger in performing the act. Whether or not he experienced symptoms in performing this act and other similar acts, he is being convinced more and more that the movement of the muscles will overcome the defeatist babble of the brain. If he did get symptoms on the way to the store but kept on going regardless, that's endorsable. Also, while in the store, he experienced symptoms, and he did not run out and abandon his objective. That is also endorsable. The first act (going to the store) was accomplished by movement of the muscles. And the second act (staying in the store) was accomplished by resolutely giving a strong command to the muscles not to move (run out and abandon the shopping), but to remain there and finish the shopping. Both these acts should be endorsed by the individual and not taken for granted.

Inner and outer environment

Our inner environment is what we can control. It is everything that is within our physical being, which includes our thoughts consisting of secure and insecure thoughts, what we say or don't say (speech muscles), what we feel, and our emotions, which can bring on symptoms and sensations that could be good, bad or indifferent.

Our outer environment is everything that is outside our inner environment which we cannot control. It includes people, places, the past, future and everything else outside ourselves.

Inner and outer approval

People, in general, have an abiding taste for receiving approval from others, to be recognized and possibly rewarded for doing something which is appreciated, a thank you, a pat on the back for a job well done, and many other complimentary gestures. It is average to want to receive gratitude for doing something that is good and recognized by others.

Wanting it, liking it, enjoying it is fine, but needing it is something else. Feeling and anticipating that we have to get it can be detrimental to our mental health. Learning the difference between subjective wants and objective needs is crucial to the nervous patient. To survive and go on living we "need" to eat and drink. To enjoy what we eat and drink, we can spice it up and flavor it. This is considered a "want." To the individual who suffers, this is important to understand. It must also be practiced. When practiced, the individual should endorse himself. Here, again, is an opportunity to humble oneself. It is important to know that seeking our own inner approval is far more important than all the outer approvals we might get from countless others.

Exceptionality

Exceptionality can be misleading to the person who is suffering. To him nothing less than average is accepted; it must be above and beyond. In most cases, he feels he is above average and that we should be. Because of this kind of thinking, he develops a fear of being below average. Goals are set beyond reason. These goals must be met and if they are not, it becomes a major problem. "What's wrong with me?" the person exclaims, "Can't I do anything right?" He feels he always has to perform in an exceptional manner. He must learn that it's okay to be average and that's what most people are. Having to perform with perfection all the time is unrealistic. There is nothing wrong with wanting to be exceptional and doing a perfect job; at times it does turn out that way. The problem only develops when the person sets these high standards for himself with the expectation that he will perform perfectly all the time. Functioning in extremes is what he does all too often (it's either magnificent or it's a total disaster). The extremes bring on excitement, whether good or bad. To the individual who suffers nervous symptoms, too much excitement can only do harm to his mental health. It is good to know that one can lower his standards and expectations at times for the sake of his mental health. And when he does, his performance will rise.

## AN OASIS IN THE WILDERNESS

Having the courage to make mistakes

Remember the old line about a philosopher who said: "I've never made a mistake in my whole entire life, although one time I thought I did, but I was mistaken." (Humor is our best friend, temper our worst enemy.)

This item could have been included under "Exceptionality." However, it is singled out here because of its relative importance. How do we tolerate making mistakes? The simple answer is, knowing other people also make mistakes in everyday life, not just us. Common sense tells us that we are going to make mistakes. Not expecting to make them now and then is a form of exceptionality (see above). A simple way to accept making mistakes is to know and observe others when they make them. We seem to tolerate and accept their mistakes better than we do ours. We tell others, "That's okay, don't worry about it, we all make mistakes." If we can tell others, then why can't we apply the same reasoning to ourselves? It is imperative to be humble in admitting that we, too, can make mistakes just like anyone else. We have to curtail worrying about what others are thinking about us. It's far more important to seek our own inner approval rather than seeking it from outer environment. We can develop humility and when we do, humility will lead us back to the road of inner peace.

Partial and total viewpoints

We've all been through situations where something has gone wrong and others where things have gone right. Unfortunately, we had focused on the things that have gone wrong (a partial viewpoint), and not on those that have gone right (taken together, a total viewpoint). What happens is that a judgment is made on who did the wrong. This judgment might be directed at oneself or at someone else. If the judgment is based entirely on the negative side (temper blocks reason and logic), then it is not assessed properly. This is where the total viewpoint comes in. Taking a broader, objective view, we are now allowing for positive views to enter the picture. When this is done, a fairer and healthier assessment can be made.

Attacking the weakest link

In the beginning of learning the Recovery Method one is made aware of how to go about doing the things he fears and hates to do to get well. If there are some things that bother us more than others, those would be considered "strong links." Those that bother us the least are considered "weak links." By attacking the weaker links first, it's more likely we will be able to handle them. Attacking the stronger links first could jeopardize the progress that has been made in getting well and discourage us from going any further. Here's an example. If one is going to a gym to work on lifting weights, he would start with the lighter ones first and as he progressed, he would then increase the amount of weights. The same holds true with mental health. When we make the effort to work on the weaker links first and continue to succeed, the once-stronger links will not seem that strong any longer. And each and every time we practice attacking the weakest link, it's important to endorse ourselves.

Observing and interpreting

Observing something and interpreting it can very easily be mistaken. It's common for people, in general, to say or do something and have it be misinterpreted by others. For those who are dealing with mental health issues it becomes important to understand how simple this is. Once he learns this, he can work on being careful not to jump to assumptions or conclusions. If he is not sure what to make out of a remark or an event, he can simply put it in its proper place of knowing he did not know. If he would like clarification, he can ask for it in a friendly manner. Too often, temper enters the picture, and temper has a way of blocking reason and logic. Remove the temper and reason and logic will be restored.

There are no rights or wrongs

One of the principles in RM is that there are no rights or wrongs in the trivialities of everyday life. Even in a court of law, they are solely based on opinions of a judge or jury. These right or wrong arguments are referred to in RM as "symbolic victories." And to a person dealing with mental health issues who can't afford the luxury of temper, it becomes an empty victory. There are no winners here, only victims, especially the patient. The thinking usually is, "You gave in," and giving in is a sign of weakness. Contrary to that type of philosophy, it is not a weakness but quite the opposite. The act of lowering your arms and choosing peace over power is far more courageous. When a patient is trained using a try-and-fail, try-and-fail-till-you-succeed method, good mental health is not too far away. To go a step further, this is not to say that one can't express his feelings. He can, but he learns to do so in a more cultured manner.

Self-spotting and foreign spotting

Foreign spotting consists of seeing the faults of others more readily than one's own, and being quick to make judgments. Alternatively, self-spotting is seldom thought of or practiced upon oneself. If one is willing to change for the sake of his mental health, it's imperative for him to learn the art of self-spotting. Looking into himself and finding his own faults can be difficult, but it can be accomplished. Also, as well as finding faults, some patients don't even find the good side or more positive side of themselves. It comes down to finding the correct balance. For a client, patient or consumer it's an essential item to learn if one desires to become well and regain his mental health. Maintaining peace, order and balance are key items on the road to recovery.

# ABOUT THE AUTHOR

Tony Ferrigno grew up in Coney Island, Brooklyn, New York. He graduated from William E. Grady Vocational High School in Brooklyn, learning a trade in woodworking and later joined the Army. After completing active duty, Ferrigno worked for the New York City Transit Authority as an ironworker's helper and later as an ironworker. He then transferred to the Department of Transportation, also as an ironworker, retiring on disability thirteen years later.

If you, or someone else you may know, would like to attend Recovery International (RI) meetings or would kindly like to make a much appreciated contribution to the RI organization or to inquire about any other information you may be interested in, please write to:

Recovery International
1415 W. 22nd Street
Tower Floor
Oak Brook, IL. 60523
Or Call: 312-337-5661 Toll free: 866-221-0302
Go online at: www.recoveryinternational.org
Email: info@recoveryinternational.org